BOOKCLUB'S

PUTS FICTION TO SHAME*

"Dramatizes a true life spy story that puts fiction to shame"

—ALLENTOWN CALL, PENNSYLVANIA

"Compelling reading"

—BUFFALO COURIER EXPRESS

"Elie Cohn made the spies of fiction look like amateurs"

—NATIONAL JEWISH MONTHLY

"Recommended"

—LIBRARY JOURNAL

OUR MAN IN DAMASCUS: ELIE COHN

by Eli Ben-Hanan

STEIMATZKY MEANS BOOKS

STEIMATZKY HOUSE:
11, HAKISHON ST., P.O.B 1444 BNEI BRAK 51114, ISRAEL

This book is dedicated to the memory of a man of great accomplishment, no longer with us, and to his wife (may she live long and happily) whose personality contributed so much to his extraordinary accomplishments.

Foreword

This book is based on facts and events which took place on the dates and in the places indicated.

The dialogs and some of the names have been changed in order to complete the picture, and so as not to prejudice persons still living among us.

I have no doubt that all this book reveals about the personality and deeds of Elie Cohn, Our Man in Damascus, is merely a drop in the ocean of his outstanding achievements; the rest we will learn only years from now, if at all.

—ELI BEN-HANAN

Preface

I knew, something inside of me whispered, that the day my
husband would become a public personality was rapidly approaching.

I said good-bye to him in the last days of November, 1964,
with a clear feeling that this would be our last meeting. When
they informed me two months later that he had been caught
—my heart ached, but I was not surprised.

"Your husband was a hero," they said in May. "His exploits will go down in history."

When the Six-Day War ended I knew that indeed that's
what he was, and now I see that history will also remember
him.

To you, the writers of history—my thanks.

—NADIA COHN

"Against the Arab you mustn't defend yourself. You have to attack . . ."
—ELIE COHN

1

The End and the Beginning

Powerful arms grasped him by the elbows and dragged him off to his cell.

His senses were numb and when they tossed him inside his head struck the concrete floor and a stream of blood streamed from his forehead. Elie Cohn gave a feeble groan and passed out.

"The swine," grumbled one of the guards. "Nothing works. He'll never open his mouth."

"Don't worry, Lieutenant," said the other guard. "A few electric treatments and a couple of swings in the cradle and he'll be singing like a bird."

The lieutenant went up to the prisoner, pulled him over on his back, and wiped the blood from his face with a rag soaked in alcohol.

"Tie him up good, Hatif, and don't let him get any rest tonight. Let him sleep on the cold floor, without mattress and blankets; in the morning you'll see how he's going to talk."

"Leave him to me. He'll talk."

The lieutenant got up and started to leave the bleak cell. When he reached the door he stopped for a moment and looked back.

"Hatif," he said. "I'm relying on you. But don't get overenthusiastic. The brass want him in good shape for the trial."

7

Hatif smiled. "Don't worry," he said. "I'll handle him with kid gloves."

Then the two of them went out and Hatif slammed the door brusquely.

Elie Cohn lay twisted on the floor, groaning quietly. The blow to his head had not increased the pain. On the contrary, it had shaken him out of his enforced apathy, that apathy for defense purposes that he had been taught in Tel Aviv.

When he opened his eyes a pain shot, like a dazzling light, into his brain. But after a few moments he got used to it and lay quiet. His legs felt like two sticks of ice and his nostrils filled with the sour, fetid smell of dry rot mixed with urine. He wanted to finger the bruise he received when he fell, but his hands were tied behind his back and linked to his legs by a chain.

His circulation had stopped, which explained why he felt so cold. He tried to raise his head to examine his situation, but the slightest movement tightened the steel chain and pulled back his shoulders. The pain was excruciating.

For a moment he decided to forego all effort and stay where he was, perhaps even to go to sleep for an hour or two. But the cold made sleep impossible.

"No," he stammered to himself. "I cannot do it."

He fixed his eyes on the peeling wall in front of him and his thoughts darted rapidly. When his head cleared he suddenly noticed that his chest was rising and falling convulsively. Each time he inhaled he got a stabbing pain in his right side.

A few minutes later he discovered he could dispel the pain, or at least weaken it, by breathing carefully and filling his lungs only halfway full.

"Remember!" Yitzhak's voice suddenly rang in his ears. "Everything you learn here may come in handy someday. Take it seriously." Yitzhak's face had grown grim for a moment. Then he added, "Let's hope you never have occasion to see that I'm right."

Elie Cohn knew the boss had been right. Now more than ever before.

There was no sense denying the fact that he was an Israeli agent. He smiled when he remembered the moments that had led him to the fateful decision.

As he lay there—bound and paining and cold—everything came back to him like a stark detective movie.

It all began casually on a spring morning in 1960, when he was working as an accountant in the Supply Department of Central Distributors.

That morning someone had knocked on the door of his office and asked if he could come in.

"Please do. Have a seat," Elie said, motioning to a chair beside his desk.

The man nodded agreeably. Then he put out his hand.

"My name is Zalman. The second name is not important." He smiled at Elie's look of amazement.

"I don't know if I can speak here," he whispered, leaning forward. "I work for the Ministry of Defense. I am an Intelligence officer."

"Intelligence officer?"

The man nodded. "It's a rather unusual job, which involves a lot of traveling. I'd say it's rather interesting."

"What do you want from *me?*" Elie asked.

"I've been asked to offer you a position in our service," the man said placidly.

"What kind of position?"

"Interesting work, which includes trips to Europe. Most likely you'll get to visit Arab countries as well."

Elie was silent for a moment.

"I'm afraid I won't be able to accept your offer," he said. "You probably know that I recently got married. I want to stay with my wife. Besides, I've had enough wandering to last me three lifetimes."

"Even if we double your present salary?"

Elie shook his head. "It won't help. I get along with what I have."

The man got up and shook hands politely. At the door he turned and said, "Thank you for giving me a few minutes of your time. I don't want to force anything on you. In any case, try to forget me and don't tell anyone of my visit. Not even your wife, Nadia."

Elie nodded.

"I understand. You can trust me."

After the man left, Elie spent a long time in thought. No doubt his visitor knew a good deal about him. The fact that he had mentioned his wife's name said a lot.

Later he tried to forget the whole affair. When he came home that evening he did not mention the meeting to anyone.

Elie Cohn's life went on as usual.

Three, four weeks passed after that curious conversation in Elie's office. On the tenth of the month, as usual, he got his paycheck; with it, though, was an envelope. He quickly ripped it open and found this notice:

As a result of cutbacks in the departments of Central Distributors, the management is compelled to dismiss you along with five other experienced employees. Thank you for your devoted service. We hope that the day we again expand our staff, we will see you in our ranks once again.

Elie blinked, and a strange gleam came into his eyes. Once again within a short period he was jobless. The burden of supporting the family would again fall on Nadia.

He went down the stairs and out into the noisy street. True, he had been given a ten-day extension, but as far as he was concerned it was the end.

From that day on Elie was not the same man. He became immersed in himself—abstracted, brooding about the host of practical problems he faced. Nadia tried not to trouble him with unnecessary questions. She knew what was bothering him.

Two days later, he was leaning over his electric calculating machine, when Zalman appeared in the doorway again.

"Good morning, Mr. Cohn," he said. "May I sit down?"

Elie extended his hands in invitation.

Zalman came to the point at once. "You probably think we've been impolite and interrupted your work here in order to make you work for us."

Elie did not answer.

"Well, the truth is that I heard about it only yesterday and by accident, and decided to come to your assistance. You understand that the Ministry of Defense does not have to have five people fired in this department to force you to work for us. But my offer still stands."

Elie lifted his hands.

"All right, Mr. Zalman. There's no need to apologize. Our world and our lives are controlled by a combination of coincidences. I'm afraid you've come at the right time."

"I'm certain that your new position will satisfy you, and your wife will be able to quit working. We'll pay you 350 pounds a month. We'll teach you the trade, and then you can take it or leave it, as you wish. In questions of conscience no one can apply pressure."

"You're repeating yourself, Mr. Zalman," Elie said. "I already told you I accept!"

Zalman got up.

"Well, we'll contact you within the next few days. Until then, treat this conversation as if it never took place."

The notice to begin work on his new job was given over the phone. "Come to the center on Allenby Street tomorrow at seven, and find some cover for what you're doing," the voice on the other end said. "Try to think of something convincing. The preparations are likely to take a few weeks."

Elie replaced the receiver. Then he stretched back in the padded chair. For a minute he played with the ivory keys of the electric calculating machine, and smiled at the result.

The next morning he kissed his wife good-bye before leaving.

"When do you think you'll be back?" Nadia asked.

Elie shrugged.

"I know when I'm going out. It's hard to say when I'll be back. They said they had an interesting job outside the city. It'll take a bit of time."

She blew him a kiss and Elie hurried down the street to catch the bus for Tel Aviv.

Not far from the central post office on Allenby Street, on the second floor of a faded lemon-colored building two men waited for this first interview.

Elie looked around. The office seemed like a thousand others he had seen. The clerks reminded him of those in any bank or similar institution. Even the girls were familiar types. All the fertile imagination he had activated for his fateful encounter with the mysterious Ministry of Defense had evaporated the minute he entered.

Someone came up to Elie and invited him into one of the rooms on the second floor. Elie went in and met a friendly chap with a high forehead and deep blue eyes. The man shook his hand heartily and introduced himself.

"Yitzhak. That's the name. It just so happens it's my real one."

Elie smiled.

"Unfortunately, we have to be terribly practical around here. So you'll forgive me if I don't prepare the background for what you'll be learning and doing here, but get right down to business."

He got up, walked over to the cabinet behind him, and took out a number of common objects. Then he tossed them on the table and said briefly: "First I'd like to give you a little aptitude test, one which you probably had in childhood."

He watched the effect of these words on Elie and then continued. "Here are a number of objects. Observe them for one minute, then close your eyes and try to recall what you've seen."

Elie looked at the objects scattered haphazardly on the table.

There was a pencil, an eraser, pins, paperclips, and a few other everyday office items. He shut his eyes and read off from memory what he had seen.

Yitzhak, who sat facing him, was highly impressed. Not only had Elie remembered every item, but he had even been able to state its location on the table.

"Your memory is phenomenal," Yitzhak stated. "Did you inherit it?"

"Perhaps," Elie said, shrugging. He recalled that as a child he was in the habit of remembering lists of things and surprising his playmates with his amazing powers. Often a quick glance at a passing car would be enough for him to recognize the make and year.

From then on Yitzhak asked him to make a mental note of documents, everyday scenes, and any suspicious activity around him.

When he passed the first test with flying colors, Yitzhak suggested that they take a walk through the streets of Tel Aviv.

"To be able to blend in with a crowd is one of the chief characteristics of a good spy," he said as they were walking.

Elie eyed him curiously. "What do you mean?"

Yitzhak waited a moment, glanced to either side, and then said in a whisper: "The moment we left the office two men came out and started following us. Even if they were standing in front of you here, at the bus stop, or in front of that shop window, you wouldn't be able to spot them. They don't look like secret service agents and they're not carrying anything that could give away their identity. But they've been tailing us ever since we left the building."

Elie looked around searchingly, but could see no one among the hurrying passersby watching them.

"Are you sure someone's following us? Right now?" he asked.

"Two persons, to be exact," Yitzhak said.

"How can I spot them in all this crowd?"

"It's simple. Stop and look in a window to see if someone stops opposite you or looks in your direction. You can also do this at the bus stop, while you read your evening paper, or at a newsstand. That's the classic method."

Elie nodded.

The mysterious world of espionage was no less real than the detective novels he had read.

He went to the newsstand across the street, bought an evening paper, and pretended to be busy reading. Out of the corner of his eye he spotted a tall character with wavy hair who flashed him a quick glance and then slipped away into a corner.

Elie smiled in satisfaction.

That was one of them. He tried to locate the other but without success.

Back at the office, Yitzhak asked Elie if he had identified the men.

"I think I spotted one of them," he said, a quiver of pride in his voice. "The tall fellow with wavy hair. But where was the other?"

Yitzhak spread out a series of photos taken with a Praktina camera as they were walking in the street.

"These pictures," he explained, "were taken with a special microfilm camera and developed on the spot. Take a good look. Here you're smiling in surprise, apparently looking for the two men. Here you're reading the paper, but your eyes are looking out for someone. Now have a good look at this one," Yitzhak said, taking a magnifying glass out of the drawer. "The man standing beside you reading the paper is the guy you're looking for."

Elie opened his eyes wide.

"You sure that's him?"

Yitzhak chuckled.

"He should be back in another ten minutes. It'll be a pleasure to introduce you."

2

Agent 088

It was the lunch break.

Elie stayed in the office and munched the sandwiches he had brought from home. He ate with gusto. The new job excited him. He was starting to like the espionage business. The first day at least.

After lunch Elie was summoned to the office of the code man, a fellow by the name of Yehuda, who was to teach him something of the theory of clandestine broadcasting, document coding, and other techniques of communication. Elie was especially interested in everything connected with codes operating according to predetermined systems.

"You don't have to remember everything by heart," Yehuda told him. "At least not in the first stage. I hear you have a remarkable memory. That's good. Because in this system of broadcasting, even the slightest error can be disastrous for both sides."

He pulled out a thick, leather-bound book from his desk drawer.

"Have a look at this. It's a list of one-time code tables you'll be given when the time comes. There's a parallel book at Headquarters.

"When you code a message, you first have to transcribe it in a fixed numerical code, which you will memorize. Then you'll destroy it. To destroy code tables we have a special chemical substance consisting of a mixture of metallic potassium and metallic sodium; it ignites on contact with water. The message coded by memory is then recorded on a tape machine connected to the transmitter. When the transmitter is switched on the tape starts turning, and the recorded message is transmitted automatically."

Elie scrutinized the code tables closely, wrinkled his forehead, and tried to understand how they worked.

For the moment the explanation was recorded in his memory. Later on, he thought, he would sit down and analyze it, step by step.

"If I understand you correctly, by coding a message · like this I can create meaningless sentences and then give them meaning by using a fixed numerical code," he said.

Yehuda nodded. "You're the first person who's managed to get the idea after one lesson."

Elie smiled broadly.

"What are you grinning about?"

"The truth is I don't understand a damn thing. But I once learned that if you think about confusing things in a manner just as confusing, people think you understand it. Isn't that funny?"

Yehuda grimaced.

"No. Not at all," he growled.

As Elie's first day of training came to a close, Yitzhak came up to him and said, "I want to see you in my office early tomorrow morning. You can tell your wife you got a job in the Ministry of Defense, but you'd better not say anything more than that."

As the days went by Elie went through a series of sports tests, medical checkups, and exercises designed to test his endurance under every conceivable situation. Often he was deliberately flunked by his employers, but generally his performance earned their full approval. He was one of the outstanding trainees, and there was nothing to prevent him from becoming the best of them all.

Then, after two months of exhaustive training, the fateful day arrived.

Elie was summoned to Yitzhak's office, where in the presence of two of the boss's assistants he was told: "As you realize, you've completed most your training. You've acquired a great deal of useful knowledge and shown a phenomenal sense of orientation." Yitzhak paused. "Now comes the big test."

Elie scratched his head.

"Is there any reason why I should be apprehensive about this?"

"To a large extent it depends on you," Yitzhak said. "Not far from here, at a travel agency, the address of which Shim'on will give you later, you'll meet a young secretary by the name of Marcelle. After you identify yourself by a prearranged sign, she will hand you a French passport issued in the name of an Egyptian Jew who emigrated to South Africa and is here on a visit to Israel.

"With this passport you will go to Jerusalem, by any means you choose. You'll remain there ten days. You'll speak French and Arabic only. And, of course, you'll have to get accustomed to your new identity. From now on your name will be Marcel Couban.

"Don't forget that you're a tourist and have a different name. If someone recognizes you, try not to get excited. Tell him he's mistaken, and continue as if nothing had happened. Like any other tourist, try to make contacts. Meet people and make them like you. And always keep in mind that you may be followed. Carelessness on your part is liable to flunk you."

Elie nodded. "When do I begin?"

"Tomorrow morning, Agent 088. Tomorrow morning."

Elie smiled and turned to go. At the door he stopped.

"Excuse me. I completely forgot," he said in a soft voice. "As you probably know, my wife is in her ninth month. Couldn't we wait till after she has the baby?"

"Births are unreliable. You may have to wait a day, a week, or even a month. We can't delay the whole operation until she gives birth."

Elie shrugged helplessly and opened the door.

Yitzhak hurried after him and tapped him affectionately on the shoulder.

"We'll contact you the moment we know whether it's a boy or a girl. Get going and stop thinking like a midwife. Nature runs its course with or without a father's moral support."

When he got home that day, earlier than usual, Nadia was in the kitchen making supper.

He came up to her from behind and kissed the back of her neck. Then he turned her around, looked at her abdomen, and began shaking his head slowly.

"When do you think it'll be over, Nadia?"

She smiled and ran her hand over her belly.

"I hope you'll be a father by the end of the month."

"This time keep your promise! For two weeks you've been telling me you'll make me a father but I'm still only a husband."

She ran her long fingers through his wavy hair.

"Don't worry, Elie. I want it to come a whole lot faster than you think. Did you ever try to imagine what it's like to carry something like this around inside of you?"

He shrugged.

"It's hard for a man to imagine."

He went into the bedroom and tossed a few shirts and a couple of changes of underwear into a small suitcase. Afterward, when they sat down at table, he decided to tell her his plans.

"Tomorrow I'm going to Jerusalem. I have to make some arrangements there, and I don't think I'll be able to be back before I finish."

He looked at her face and at her brown eyes.

"I wanted very much to be with you at this time. But there's no choice."

Nadia stabbed the meat with her fork.

"You're not saying anything?"

"What do you want me to say?" she asked, her voice choked with grief. "Do you want me to cry to keep you here with me?"

"You're exaggerating. It'll be a week or ten days. Mother will come to help you, and I'll be back in time for the birth of our son."

"Couldn't you get a few days' leave?"

"They've promised me some time off as soon as I finish the job in Jerusalem," he said, trying to soothe her.

Nadia said nothing and they continued eating in silence.

The next morning, earlier than usual, Elie made his way to the taxi stand. A taxi, he said to himself, would strengthen the impression of a well-to-do tourist.

On the way to the capital he thought about the recent past. It was strange, the way he had happened onto the world of espionage, how he had chosen this dangerous and intriguing profession.

Though he did not know exactly where they were planning to send him, he suspected that at the end of his training he'd be assigned as an agent to one of the Arab countries.

He hoped it would be Egypt. There the risk was greatest, but there too he had once had friends, and if he was going to take risks—he said to himself—then at least let it be on the altar of revenge.

Through his mind flashed kaleidoscopic scenes from the nineteen fifties, the time of trial of the Martyrs of Cairo.

It had happened at the end of the summer of 1954.

Information arriving from London caused Israeli leaders a considerable amount of worry. It seemed that the elderly Churchill—under Egyptian pressure and pressured by frequent acts of terrorism—had decided to withdraw the British forces from their bases in the Suez Canal area.

For the ruling junta in Egypt this was a considerable accomplishment, but as far as Israel was concerned the British presence in the canal area was vital.

It was clear to the Israeli Government that as long as the British remained there they occupied the attention of the Arab masses, and served as the target for all their undirected hatred and energy. The more official reason was that the British presence in such a potentially inflammable area would likely cool down Egypt's hawks, especially those officers thinking out loud about a "second round" in the war with Israel.

The best solution seemed to be a series of sabotage attempts and open provocations, to be carried out by hired terrorists, secretly trained in sabotage and espionage since 1951 by Israeli agents.

Some of the terrorists had even received "scholarships" for advanced training in Israel, which they had reached via France.

Among those who came to Israel were two of Elie Cohn's good friends—the dentist Ezra Marzouk and the teacher Shmuel Azar. After extensive training they returned to Egypt, where they worked in coordination with the Israeli agents Avraham (John Darling) Dar and Dr. Max Benet.

This underground nucleus attracted a group of inexperienced but patriotic Jewish youths. None of them was over thirty, and they were divided into two groups, one in Cairo, the other in Alexandria.

The men, who knew one another, were well aware of the importance of their task. If any one of them was caught, the entire outfit would collapse like a house of cards.

Elie Cohn knew about the organization. He had even assisted it, though indirectly.

Then, in the months of May and June, 1954, Israel decided to activate the group decisively. Instructions were received at the headquarters calling for sabotage in public buildings, cinemas, post offices, and railroad stations.

The main target was to be British institutions such as libraries, cultural centers, houses owned by British citizens, and the British legation in Egypt. The aim? To bring Britain to the conclusion that it was still too early to pull out of Egypt and that all the guarantees offered by the Egyptian Government in exchange for the evacuation of the bases were ineffective in the light of the continuing wave of terrorism.

In the middle of July the fateful message arrived, and Operation Egypt began.

At that very moment, however, the terrorism was already at its height, and Egyptian Intelligence was already on the trail of the saboteurs. The collapse of the network was only a matter of time.

On the same day simple explosive charges, in Vim soap-flake boxes, went off in the post office and a luggage storage room.

Two days later, on July 14, fires broke out in the United States Information Service Offices in Cairo and Alexandria and in the Embassy and Consulate in Cairo. Though the damage was light, it resulted in an international scandal.

That evening, Headquarters decided on a twenty-four-hour break in hostilities. The directives expected from Israel had not yet arrived, and Headquarters didn't want to take responsibility for the cataclysm that would likely ensue. Moreover, the Egyptian Intelligence and the police had made widespread arrests, and were beginning to show signs of impatience.

A twenty-four-hour cease-fire was essential.

Twenty hours later, on July 16, following the strongly worded American protest, a second wave was begun. The Cairo group destroyed several public buildings, while the Alexandria group agreed to blow up two cinemas, the Rivoli and the Rio.

The fact that Egyptian Intelligence was guarding all public buildings in these cities did not serve as a deterring factor. That day, however, the group's daring and rashness worked against them.

In the plaza, in front of the Rio Cinema in Alexandria, a young man with European features collapsed in agony. A security agent standing nearby noticed smoke coming out of his pocket. It was a most unusual sight, by any standards, and especially for a suspicious security agent.

He rushed over and pulled an eyeglass case full of smoldering, blackened material out of the young man's pocket. The man smiled in satisfaction.

"What's your name, boy?" he asked.

"Philip Nathanson."

"Okay, Philip," the officer said, "come and join me down at the station. I think they're expecting you, and your friends too."

Philip got up and was dragged to the police station.

"Here's one of them." the Intelligence man exclaimed.

"Check this material. I think it's a homemade bomb that went off too early."

The police lab report confirmed this.

"Look here, Philip," the officer said. "Nothing is hidden from us. I'm glad we've managed to catch you. As an Egyptian patriot I'm proud that I've prevented you from carrying out an act of terrorism. And now we'll take care of your friends in Cairo too."

He questioned the lad thoroughly, then asked: "Tell me, why have your sabotage attempts been directed against Western embassies and institutions?"

"As Egyptian patriots, we want to get the foreign agents out of our country," Nathanson said. "They won't go unless we give them a shove."

The officer chuckled.

"Who told you that 'shoves' like that will get the British out of Egypt?"

"Well," he replied, after a short hesitation, "it worked in Palestine. There they gave the British so much trouble that they had to leave."

The officer guffawed.

"If I'm supposed to believe you're really an Egyptian patriot, how do you explain the fact that you and your friends have blown up cinemas and post offices, which are Egyptian property?"

Nathanson shrugged. "Those weren't serious explosions."

"Serious or not," the officer retorted, "they were explosions."

"True. But we had to practice on something."

In the course of the interrogation, which wasn't carried out with kid gloves, the entire group was revealed. Following Nathanson's arrest, another eleven persons were taken into custody, among them an intelligent and beautiful Jewish girl from Cairo, sports champion Victoria (Marcelle) Ninio.

Heading the list of detainees were three of the ringleaders: Cairo dentist Dr. Ezra Marzouk, teacher Shmuel Azar, and Dr. Max Benet, the instructor in espionage. The only one who managed to evade the Egyptian dragnet was Israeli agent Avraham Dar, also known as John Darling.

The day of the manhunt, Elie Cohn returned home as if nothing had happened. On the way he met a friend, an Egyptian police officer, who told him with the utmost secrecy that several Israeli terrorists had been arrested.

"One of them," Elie remembered the man saying, "is Dr. Marzouk."

There was little choice. He hurried home and destroyed the secret documents in the attic. Then he hid the revolver.

Something told him they would soon be coming for him. And indeed, less than twelve hours later two policemen knocked on his door.

"Elie Cohn?" they asked.

"That's the name," he answered, and went along with them.

The police did not succeed in incriminating him and he went free from lack of evidence. Nevertheless, his name and photo were filed in the album of suspects.

From then on, he knew, he could be rearrested anytime they chose. But as a Jew he must accept his fate and show courage.

The torture machine in Cairo Prison began working. Under relentless cross-examination every one of the suspects collapsed. Max Benet broke down completely. He slashed his veins on a nail in the cell door and bled to death.

Three months after the arrests the first item on the capture of the Israeli spy network appeared in the Egyptian press.

The trial itself was set for December 17th.

As soon as the trial was announced, requests for clemency began to pour in from all parts of the world. They came, from among others, the Chief Rabbi of Egypt, the American and British Ambassadors, the Papal Nuncio, the French Foreign Minister, and the British Labour Members of Parliament.

All this, apparently, didn't help.

The trial lasted thirty days and on January 17, 1955, the court handed down its verdict. Two suspects were acquitted, two sentenced to seven years' imprisonment, two to life imprisonment, and the ringleaders, Dr. Marzouk and Shmuel Azar, were sentenced to death.

Elie tried to meet with them, but they were allowed no visitors. At dawn on January 21, 1955, they were led out and hanged in the main yard of the prison, in the presence of a few eyewitnesses.

The picture of the two—with the rope around their necks —was splashed across the front pages of next morning's papers.

Elie Cohn's heart ached at the fate of his friends. But at the same time he knew the day of revenge would come.

3

Training Missions

In the taxi on the way to Jerusalem, traveling under an assumed identity and practicing for an espionage job in one of the Arab countries, Elie felt that day of vengeance fast approaching.

He looked around him. Sha'ar Haggai. Here and there lay the scorched steel skeletons left from the convoy that had broken through to Jerusalem in the War of Independence.

His thoughts were interrupted as the car slowed down on the hill to the Castel. In the distance, beyond the sun-gilded hills, he could see Jerusalem.

"Driver, do you speak French?" Elie asked.

The driver turned to him. "So-so. I can speak English and Arabic. My French isn't so good."

"Good, then I'll speak Arabic," Elie said, and asked him where the King David Hotel was.

"When we get to the center of town I'll show you how to get there," the driver said. "You from Morocco?"

"No. Egypt. But I've been in France for several years."

"That's what I thought. You speak Arabic like an Egyptian, not a Moroccan."

Not far from the entrance to the city they passed Binyenei Ha-Ooma, the Jerusalem Concert Hall. Then they came to Yafo Street and the gates of the Knesset building.

"You staying at the King David?" the driver asked politely.

"Uh-huh."

"I'll take you there, special."

He brought Elie to the door of the hotel. Though they hadn't set a price for the special trip, Elie reckoned he didn't have more than two Israeli pounds coming.

He handed the cabby the money and thanked him.

The driver looked at the two pounds and said to himself in Hebrew, "Skinflint, just like all the Israelis."

Elie smiled to himself. He realized he'd have to be more generous if he wanted to make people like him. The budget alloted him for the ten days was something like six hundred pounds.

The King David Hotel was a watering place for people of the top echelons. In the elegant lobby contacts and acquaintances were made, and conversations on matters of high policy and business meetings were held. A great variety of people from every corner of the world preferred the place to other hotels.

The hotel's windows looked out on a typical Jerusalem landscape, and the entire building was a blend of luxuries pervaded with a warm and intimate atmosphere.

The reception clerk turned the register around, and Elie signed his new name as listed in his passport.

The clerk then gave Elie the key to his room on the second floor.

Elie entered the clean, well-appointed room and removed his warm suit and wet shirt. He preferred a trico sport shirt, which suited him better.

The large mirror on the closet door filled up with his image when he went to hang up his clothes. His masquerade as a tourist had succeeded well, at least so far.

He looked at his watch. It was ten past eleven. The sun was high in the sky, and figuring it was no time to go out, he lay down and took a nap on the comfortable bed.

Around two o'clock there was a knock on the door. Elie rose quickly and opened it.

One of the hotel clerks was standing in the doorway. "For you, sir," he said, handing Elie a sealed telegram.

A. 088
  Till now you've been brilliant. Mix in society and try to make contacts.

                                        Y—

Elie crumpled the telegram and tossed it into the wastepaper basket.

Y. could wait a few hours, he said to himself. I need some sleep if I want to stay awake tonight.

At five he went down to have supper, and afterward, feeling fit and full, he went back to his room to shower and dress.

He planned to take in a movie and then a nightclub. He would try to meet students or people in higher positions.

His well-groomed appearance at that hour of the evening

attracted considerable attention. He looked for all the world like a well-heeled tourist.

The movie didn't interest him especially. It was a cheap melodrama, the kind Hollywood produces a dime a dozen. He left in the middle and started walking the streets aimlessly.

Finally he hailed a taxi and decided to drive out of the city to kill time until the nightclubs opened.

"Where to, boss?" the driver asked, as they left Jerusalem.

"Go wherever you like," Elie said simply. "I'm not in any special hurry."

"This evening tour," the driver said, glancing at him through the mirror, "is going to cost a lot of money."

Elie chuckled. "You think I can't afford it?"

The driver looked at the road in front of him with satisfaction.

At the curve before the Castel, Elie spotted a car stuck by the side of the road.

"Pull over!" he ordered.

"What's up, Rothschild?"

"Maybe we can help that couple."

The driver shrugged.

"Remember, boss, it's your idea. I never argue with a passenger."

They pulled up at the side of the road not far from the car. Elie got out, introduced himself, and asked courteously if he might be of any help.

The man, who was leaning over the hood, looked up and gave him a long and careful look.

"Actually, I don't know what's wrong, so I don't know how you could help me. Besides, why should you get yourself dirty. We'll make out all right."

The taxi driver intervened. "Get in and turn on the ignition," he said with authority. "Maybe we can find out what's the matter."

The man did so, but the motor wouldn't start.

Ten minutes later, when all their efforts proved unavailing, Elie proposed that they leave the car where it was.

"You can come with me. I was going back to the city in any case."

"Please don't trouble yourself on our account," said the woman.

"I was about to return anyhow. I sometimes take trips out of the city and back again."

The man looked at him in amazement.

"By taxi?" he exclaimed. "That must cost you a fortune."

"When I'm at home it costs me a lot less. But as a tourist I have to leave a few dollars behind."

The man exchanged glances with his wife. Then he said in a low voice, "If this gentleman insists on taking us to Jerusalem, I can't see how we can refuse."

The taxi driver nodded in agreement. "I think you'd better accept his offer. It's the brighter side of our duty to be nice to tourists."

The three of them got into the taxi, which hurried back to the capital.

Elie smiled to himself with satisfaction. The boss would be happy. He had managed to make the acquaintance of a business couple, members of Jerusalem high society.

When the couple got out, he saw no sense in staying out any longer.

"Take me to the hotel," he told the driver. "I think I've had enough activity for one evening."

The next day the phone rang in his hotel room. It was the woman from the previous evening.

"Friday evening," she said, "we're having our twentieth wedding anniversary. Would you honor us with your presence?"

"But, madame," Elie said. "I don't know any of your relatives. Wouldn't I be out of place?"

"I'll see that you feel at home. Actually, most of our acquaintances are business people. You'll find a common language with them, I'm sure of it."

"Very well, since you're so kind. I'll try to be there."

She gave him the address.

"If you want you can walk it. It's only three blocks from your hotel."

That evening when Yitzhak phoned him, Elie told him that the first contact had been made.

"Excellent. It seems you're on the right track. That couple has good friends in the textile industry, and that's an area you know a little about."

"Textiles?" Elie asked.

"Yes, textiles. And you'd better learn more about it fast. The conversation will probably get around to it one way or another."

Elie chuckled. "It's a good thing I didn't fall in with a family of doctors. I'd have to learn medicine in two days."

When he got back to his hotel room after the party he found an urgent message. "Contact the office immediately."

He picked up the receiver, asked for an outside line, and then waited until he heard the voice of the boss on the other end.

"Where've you been till now?" Yitzhak roared. "We've been trying to get you for the last two hours."

"Well, you know, it was a party. I couldn't run away in the middle."

"Okay, but you're not going to sleep now. Get ready to hit the road."

Elie stood there, his legs spread apart, and stretched out his left hand to get a look at his watch under his sleeve.

"Chief," he said, "you know what time it is?"

"Of course. If you'd been two hours earlier, I might have let you sleep in the car. But now there's no time to lose. I've given orders to have you brought here by plane."

"What's the rush?"

"Better not ask," Yitzhak said. "There's a Ford waiting for you at the hotel gate. The driver'll take you to the airfield. He's wearing a black beret. He's one of us. Get moving, and don't leave him freezing out there in that lousy Jerusalem weather."

The connection was abruptly cut off.

A full minute later Elie put down the receiver. Then he donned his overcoat and went out.

The driver took him promptly to the airfield where a two-seater plane was waiting for him. He got in at once, and in a matter of moments they were moving briskly along the runway. Then the plane climbed rapidly into the dark sky.

The last lights of Jerusalem disappeared behind them. They flew over the Judean Hills and then cut across the coastal plain.

"Where are we going?" he asked the pilot.

"Haifa."

"Haifa?"

"Those are my instructions," the pilot called. "Another half hour and we'll be there."

"Where are we going to land in Haifa?"

"There's an airfield not far from the city. I can't risk landing anywhere else," the pilot explained. "Don't worry, there'll be a car waiting for you."

Elie nodded.

"Everything's all arranged."

He leaned back in the padded seat and wondered what was in store for him. His eyes closed from time to time and his face showed fatigue. They had been flying over forty minutes with a deafening engine roar. After an hour the lights of Haifa could be seen on the horizon.

A row of lights indicated the landing field. The plane made a sharp turn, inclined slightly to the right, and started heading downward. The monotonous roar of the engine gave way to a nerve-racking whine, and then the runway rushed up to meet them at an insane speed. The wheels touched down and the body shuddered for a second, then straightened out and glided placidly toward a small hangar.

When the plane stopped and the door opened, two men in heavy coats and dark hats came up and shook Elie's hand warmly.

"Come with us," they told him as soon as he got down.

"Where to?"

"You'll see."

The car was parked at the entrance to the airfield. One of the men opened the door for Elie and shoved him inside. A bit too brusquely, Elie thought.

Then the car zoomed toward Haifa along the road leading from the suburbs.

"If I didn't know who you were," Elie said in a moment of hilarity, "I'd think you were taking me to Damon Jail."

The man beside him frowned and said, "It would be better for you if you keep your mouth shut. We aren't doing this for our health."

Elie smiled. "Just between us, I think I'm starting to like this business."

The man who was driving looked at him in the mirror and muttered: "I doubt if you'll think so tomorrow morning, after you undergo a special investigation in that prison you just mentioned."

Elie's heart skipped a beat.

"What's the idea of this trip, gentlemen?" he asked, with a certain uneasiness.

"It's better if you don't know. It'll help strengthen your character."

The man beside him gave him a friendly tap on the shoulder, drew out a pack of Marlboro cigarettes, and offered him one.

"What about you?" Elie asked.

"I polished off two packs waiting for you to arrive. I have a nicotine burn in my throat."

He gave Elie a light and watched him exhale clouds of smoke. A minute later, Elie fell into a deep sleep.

When Elie awoke and realized where he was, there was a bright light shining overhead that gained several times its brightness due to the whitewashed walls.

He got to his knees and crawled over to the pitchei standing on the side. His lips felt like rubber and his eyes were rolling in their sockets.

He was about to reach out, when somebody kicked the pitcher. The water spilled out onto the floor.

"Good morning, Marcel," the man said, turning to Elie and looking him over.

"What am I doing here?" he asked.

"You've been brought here by men from the counter-intelligence department. I don't believe you'll leave here before you tell us who you are, and whom you're working for. And what you were doing in Jerusalem."

Elie tried to smile, but his cracked lips pained sharply.

"Do you think it would be possible to have a drink before we begin the interrogation?"

The man frowned.

"Don't be smart, Marcel. We had orders to kidnap and then extract every possible bit of information from you. We know you're an Egyptian merchant from South Africa here on a visit to Israel. It's clear to us you've been given a forged identity. Our men have followed you from the moment you got out of the car that brought you to Jerusalem. We have ways to make you talk."

Elie licked his lips.

"What do you want to know?"

"Who sent you to Jerusalem?"

"I came of my own free will."

"As a tourist?"

"As a tourist."

"With a forged passport?"

"That's my passport. And that's my name and statistics."

"You're lying!" one of the men snapped. "You got that passport from somebody who told you to make contacts and snoop around in the capital."

Elie shook his head.

"You're mistaken, gentlemen."

"We'll soon see who's mistaken."

The interrogator left the cell and came back directly with a hawk-faced man and another who looked like a pugilist.

"I want the interrogation started immediately," he ordered. "Put him in the bath. And make sure it's *hot* enough."

Elie was pulled to his feet and led to the bath.

"Strip!" the man ordered.

Elie stripped.

"Get into the water!"

For six minutes his teeth chattered convulsively. His body turned blue and his eyes rolled in their sockets.

"Your real name, Marcel," the man demanded.

"Marcel," Elie said through chattering teeth.

"You're wasting your own time," the interrogator said. "Ten minutes is the maximum a man can take in cold like this. Why don't you save yourself another four minutes of unpleasantness?"

Elie shook his head.

"My name's Marcel. I have no other name."

One of the men went over and whispered something to the interrogator.

"Okay," he said. "Take him out before he turns into a block of ice."

The two sturdy men took him out of the icy bath and massaged him until circulation returned.

Two hours later, Elie was taken to a second interrogation chamber, reeking of urine and excrement.

"Men who've spent only half an hour here have revealed everything," the interrogator said. "I don't believe you're an iron man."

Elie was shoved into the stinking hole while his interrogators stood on the other side and rained questions on him.

The answers were feeble and indistinct, but they contained nothing new. Elie stuck to his story. Half an hour later he was close to unconsciousness, but still had control of his mind.

The interrogation continued into the late hours of the night, and for twenty hours after that. Finally he was given a shot in the arm and transported, unconscious, all the way back to his hotel room in Jerusalem.

When he awoke from the effect of the shot, his eyes were dazzled by the daylight. For several minutes he lay without moving. Slowly he looked around and realized where he was. Nothing had changed in the room. Everything that had happened seemed like a bad nightmare.

He got up, shuffled over to the door in his bare feet, and noticed that a note had been slipped under the door.

He licked his sore lips, tore open the envelope, and read the note.

Dear A.

For the past twenty hours I've been wondering where you disappeared to. I believe you were kidnapped by the other department, one over which unfortunately I have no control. I hope that you haven't told them anything. Our man received false instructions to take you to the airfield, and then we lost contact with you. I hope you feel okay now. I'm expecting you tomorrow in my office.

Y—

Elie looked up from the letter, disappointed. Yitzhak was making fun of him and playing a double game. Maybe it was all for the best; maybe that was part of the test. But the way he did it was not at all to his liking.

His thoughts hovered a moment between reality and fantasy, and then the phone rang.

He reached out and lifted the receiver.

"Hello," he mumbled drowsily.

From the other end there was silence.

"Hello!" He tried again, but there was no reply.

Then came a metallic sound of the line being disconnected.

Now they know I'm awake, he thought to himself. I can look forward to guests or an important phone call.

He dressed quickly, shaved, and ordered breakfast sent to his room.

"Bring me double portions," he told the waiter. "I feel like tearing apart something big this morning."

"Right away, sir," the waiter said. "Right away."

After ten days in Jerusalem, Elie returned to Tel Aviv. The center was proud of his work.

"You carried out your assignment for the better," Yitzhak said with satisfaction. "I think that soon you'll be able to begin actual work, the kind that's of use to us. Till then you have ten days' leave."

"Ten days?" Elie was elated.

Yitzhak shrugged his shoulders.

"Ten days isn't such a long time to spend with your·wife and newborn daughter."

"Daughter? Thanks!" Elie said.

He was out of the office the next moment.

On his way home, Elie bought a number of toys and a gift for his wife. He was happy to be a father. For a long moment the world seemed a wonderful place to live in.

"What'll we name her?" Nadia asked him

Elie thought for a moment, then said, "Mother will be happy if we name the baby after her."

"Sophie," Nadia said quietly. "Sophie Cohn. It sounds lovely."

"It ought to be lovely. Mother will be very happy."

Elie leaned over and kissed her.

"I've got ten days' leave. We'll make up for lost time."

That same afternoon Elie was summoned to Yitzhak's office. He was given a returning hero's welcome.

"Sit down, Elie," said the man he had come to know so well. "I've invited you here to give you some idea of the plans of this bureau. As you can imagine, we haven't invested all this time and money just to make you a run-of-the-mill informant. The country's pinning great hopes on you."

"What do I have to do?"

"You'll have to get used to the fact that you're a Moslem. That in itself ought to keep you busy. You'll have to think the way a good Moslem thinks and act accordingly. Everything else will come in due course."

"You think I can pass as a Moslem?" Elie asked.

Yitzhak gave him a probing look, appraising his tall form and oriental features.

"I don't think there's the slightest doubt. You'd pass for a Moslem in every respect, even if you don't know the Koran or that Muhammad was the prophet of Allah."

After a moment of silence he added, "Incidentally, when it comes to questions of religion, remember the following rule: If they ask you questions you're not sure of, tell them you're not an orthodox Moslem and you have only vague memories from your schooldays.

"In any case"—a glimmer of a smile appeared at the corner of his mouth—"it's too early to worry. We aren't planning to toss you straight into the lions' den. You'll have your first real test in a neutral country, in the local Arab colony. Do you think you can handle it?"

Elie smiled. "Can I still back out?"

"So listen carefully. When you leave here we'll fix you up a Syrian or Iraqi identity card. When the time comes the appropriate person will give it to you."

"Why Iraq?" Elie asked. "I don't know much about Iraq. Why don't I go on a mission to Egypt? There I know my way around better."

"Can't be done," Yitzhak sighed, lighting a cigarette. "Egypt keeps a careful record of all its citizens and a list of all passports that have been issued. It's too much of a risk. In Iraq and Syria, on the other hand, they have utter chaos in the registration."

Elie nodded. "I'll go wherever you send me."

4

The First Mission

Toward the end of December preparations for Elie's first real mission got into high gear. For a spy in an Arab country there was hardly anyone more suitable or better qualified. Nevertheless, it had been decided to give Elie a trial run among the people with whom he'd be living and working.

"From now on," Yitzhak told him one morning, "your name is Kamel. Your father was Amin Tabet. Your mother's name was Sa'ida Ibrahim.

"Here's your life history: You were born in Beirut. When you were three years old, your family moved to Alexandria, Egypt. Don't forget that—your family is Syrian. A year later your sister died. Your father was a textile merchant.

"In 1946 your uncle emigrated to Argentina. A short time later he wrote and invited you to join him.

"In 1947 you came to Argentina with your family. Your ather and uncle went into partnership with a third man in a textile business in Buenos Aires, but things didn't go too well and they went bankrupt.

"Your father died in 1956 and six months later your mother also died. You went to live with your uncle. You've worked for a while in a travel agency, then went into business on your own. Naturally you were a great success."

Elie nodded.

"Before you leave," Yitzhak went on, "you'll have to prepare your family for your forthcoming trip. Think of some thing convincing like a purchasing mission for the Defense Ministry or something else that's important and can't be discussed.

"Tell them you'll be back on leave from time to time. As far as supporting them goes, we'll take care of that," he said. "Everything clear?"

"Of course."

"You can go. We'll take care of all the formalities and call you tomorrow."

He was about to leave the room when Yitzhak called, "Kamel, look at me."

Elie turned quickly.

"Very good," Yitzhak said with satisfaction. "I'm glad to see you've started to think like an Arab. Now all you need to be a hundred percent convincing is a big moustache."

Elie ran his index finger over his upper lip and made a face.

When he reached home he decided to break the news to Nadia.

"I've got a new job with a private outfit working with the Defense Ministry and the Foreign Office," he told her. "They need someone who'll go to Europe to buy certain instruments and materials for the military industries and locate markets. I'll get long vacations and I'll be back often."

He looked at her, waiting for her to say something, but she let him go on talking. He felt he had to reassure her.

"I know it's going to be hard, Nadia," he said in a soft voice. "But it won't be for long. The Ministry will take care of everything you need. They'll be sending my salary here. When I get back we'll be able to lead a much better life."

"What about the baby? Doesn't she need a father?"

"She does. But she needs a good future even more. At this stage a mother is more important to her, and when she needs me I'll be with her and her future will be assured."

"Have you told your brothers about this?" she asked.

He shook his head.

"I was thinking of doing it Saturday. Till then let's forget all about it and enjoy the time that's left."

He noticed that Nadia's eyes were wet.

"Don't cry, dear. If I could take you with me I would—believe me."

"No," she stammered in a choked voice. "I don't want to leave here. This is my country. This is my home and this is my family. It's just that I wanted my husband to be here too."

He ran his hand through her soft black hair.

"In a few more months I'll be back by your side. Forever."

At the family gathering on Saturday, Elie's brothers and the rest of the family sat down to dinner. Elie took his customary place at the head of the table and the meal proceeded to the sound of songs and laughter.

Later, when the conversation came around to everyday matters, Elie revealed the real reason for the invitation.

"I wanted to tell you that thanks to some pull I had in the
Defense Ministry, I've landed a job with a private outfit
working with the Ministry. They import and export army
equipment and they want me to be their purchasing agent in
Europe.

"I'm going to spend some time there to get to know the
score and make the right contacts. When everything's running
smoothly I'll come back and handle things from this end. Of
course, it pays very well. And Nadia and I, as I'm sure you
realize, need a larger income."

"When do you think you'll be leaving, Elie?" asked one of
the brothers.

"I'm not sure yet. Probably in another ten days or so. In
the meantime, I have to get a passport and make all the arrangements."

"Are people there not supposed to know you as you are,
Elie?" his brother Maurice asked suddenly.

Elie turned pale.

"Why do you say that, Maurice?"

"I see you're growing a moustache."

"So what?" Elie shrugged. "You don't think it suits me?"

"Mmmm. To tell you the truth, it suits you very well. But
I'm curious to know how come you're suddenly growing a
moustache when you objected to one all these years," Maurice said. "I remember you always used to say, 'What's it
good for? Who needs a soup strainer?'"

Elie chuckled.

"Right, but since then I've changed my mind. Besides,
Father always used to say that a moustache makes a man
look serious. Without a moustache I had a daughter. Now I
want a son. And if you want to be the father of a little man,
you have to look like a man, not a sissy."

Elie's departure was delayed until the beginning of February. The preparations and arrangements were all made
through the official channels to avoid undue suspicion.

When everything was ready, Elie got his final instructions.

"Tomorrow," Yitzhak told him, "you leave for Europe by
a direct flight. I wish you all the best."

The two of them shook hands warmly.

"Let's have no long-drawn-out farewells. In this business
there's no room for sentiment. Do what you have to do, Elie.
I'll be in touch with you almost daily."

Yitzhak blinked and whacked Elie affectionately on the

shoulder. He sent up a silent prayer that his protege would succeed.

Next morning a car pulled up in front of the house on Ha-tehiya Street and drove Elie to the airport.

A young escort named Gideon handed Elie his passport, issued in his real name, together with five hundred dollars and a plane ticket to Zurich, Switzerland.

"Someone will be waiting for you at Zurich airport," Gideon told him. "He'll give you further instructions."

Elie shook hands and climbed up the loading ramp.

Less than ten minutes later the plane climbed into the sky. Tel Aviv disappeared from view, and the blue-green sea occupied the entire view from the round windows.

"Ladies and gentlemen," the voice of the stewardess said over the loudspeaker. "We have just taken off from Tel Aviv. Our first stop will be Rome. Our altitude is fifteen thousand feet and our speed is 380 miles per hour. We will arrive in Rome at twelve o'clock. The captain and crew wish you a pleasant trip."

Elie looked around.

Apart from himself there were a number of elderly tourists, some businessmen, and a family with two children.

He decided to devote the rest of the trip to sleep, and when the charming stewardess came around with sandwiches and a cold drink, she found him out like a light.

She smiled to herself.

The manly passenger with the moustache was sleeping like a baby in a cradle.

When the plane was about to land she woke him up and told him to fasten his seat belt.

"We land in Rome in less than twenty minutes. Passengers will remain in their seats until refueling is completed." A short time later the plane was airborne again.

The roar of the engines ceased the moment the wheels of the giant plane touched the asphalt runway of Kloten Airport in Zurich. The door opened and the boarding ramp was brought up.

Following a few elderly passengers, Elie appeared in the doorway and surveyed the scene from behind his tinted sunglasses.

He went through customs in record time. His few pieces of luggage got white chalk marks and his passport was stamped with a big blue circle.

On the other side of the gleaming glass wall stood a man with silver hair, who identified Elie from a photo he had in his hand.

"Mr. Cohn?" he asked.

Elie nodded.

"I'm your contact here in Zurich. Give them your passport and take this one."

Elie handed over his passport, which had just been stamped with the entry visa to Zurich, and in exchange received a European passport with visas for Chile and Argentina.

"When you get to Buenos Aires, they'll contact you. The people there will see about prolonging your visa. You can spend the night in Zurich and go out on the town, and tomorrow at dawn you take off for South America. Here's your ticket for Santiago. Someone will be waiting for you at the airport."

"How do I recognize him?"

"The same way you recognized me. In other words, he'll contact you. When you get the information from him you set out straight for Buenos Aires. You're to be there no later than Wednesday. At eleven o'clock Wednesday there'll be somebody waiting for you at the Cafe Corrientes in downtown Buenos Aires."

On Wednesday at the appointed hour, Elie was at the Cafe Corrientes in Buenos Aires.

A middle-aged man with Slavic features, who introduced himself as Avraham, told him: "We've fixed you up an apartment in the central part of the city. You'll stay there while you learn to speak Spanish like a good Argentinian. I'll recommend a suitable teacher. When you know enough Spanish you can continue with your mission. As far as expenditures are concerned, in the first stage you can act freely, and later on we'll allow you to be as lavish as the job requires."

That same evening Avraham introduced the elderly lady who would be his teacher.

"Better let your other language with her be French," he said, looking at his watch. "I'll wait for you in the cafe after the lesson."

The first lesson was a lengthy one, and Avraham waited long and impatiently. Finally, he got up and went to meet him. They met half way.

"Well," Avraham muttered drily, "I thought you weren't coming."

Elie gave a meager smile.

"What's up?" he asked.

"First of all, remember you're in a transition stage. You aren't a Syrian citizen because you're holding aloof from the Syrian community here. On the other hand, you aren't a citizen of any other country, because you're carrying a Syrian passport. In this situation it's better if you don't run around too much. At least not before you master the language. And that has to come within two months' time.

"I'll get you the right papers and then you'll move into the Syrian quarter and try to mix in society. In the meantime, it's better if we don't meet. At least not in public."

"What about the apartment and my business here?"

"Try to live quietly. I'll cover all expenses. Money doesn't have to worry you. Anyway, memorize this address and then destroy it."

He handed Elie a visiting card.

"Remember, this is only in case of emergency."

For the next two months, during which Elie became proficient in Spanish, they seldom met.

Then, one bright morning Avraham said, "The time has come. I've got everything set up for your new role. Here's a Syrian passport in the name of Kamel Amin Tabet. Tomorrow you'll move into the Syrian quarter.

"I've rented an apartment for you, Calle Takuara 1485, in downtown Buenos Aires. I hope the story about your uncle and the texile business is convincing. Good luck. This mission is very important for us."

5

Important Contacts
in Argentina

The atmosphere in the Arab colony's Moslem Club in Calle France, Buenos Aires, was warm and intimate. Despite the fact that it was a relatively progressive country, Elie could still sense the men's feeling of superiority over their wives.

As he entered he saw that the people present were divided into two groups. In one corner about ten men sat conversing quietly; their wives were sitting and gossiping in another corner.

As he looked at them he noticed that one girl was not taking an active part in the conversation. She was Georgette, the young daughter of Houwari Mashhour, an old-time Syrian emigrant who held a key position in the local branch of the Esso Oil Company.

Georgette spotted him and their eyes met. She greeted him with a nod.

Her father had hinted that Georgette admired him very much. In other words, he meant to say, he wouldn't have any objection if they saw each other outside the club as well.

Elie got the hint and wasn't unduly surprised. In less than three months he had become the most sought-after bachelor in the Syrian community of Buenos Aires, which tried to avoid intermarriages.

"Good evening, Kamel," a man's voice behind him said.

He truned and saw the dwarfish figure of Latif El-Zaoumi, a club regular and a successful accountant. He was a department manager at Bong and Borne, the biggest trading company south of the equator.

"Good evening, Latif," Elie replied, courteously. "How's business?"

"Getting better every day, *insh'allah*," said the dwarfish, potbellied little man. "We have 43 million head of cattle here in Argentina, and that's enough for business to succeed, isn't it?"

"Forty-three million!" Elie cried in amazement. "Why, if

I'm not mistaken, that's twice the number of persons in Argentina."

El-Zaoumi nodded.

"While we're mentioning statistics, perhaps you'd be interested to know that one-sixth of the area of the country serves, as grazing areas and cattle-breeding ranches."

Elie raised an expression of wonder.

He knew that to win friends and influence people he had to listen patiently to what they had to say, even when it was boring as hell.

Apparently Elie was one of the few people willing to suffer El-Zaoumi's facts and figures, because he rambled on enthusiastically.

"That's not all—180,000 ranch hands are employed in cattle raising and the meat is marketed and exported by 788 companies. This past year, for example, Argentina exported 392 million dollars' worth of meat."

"Does Argentina export meat to Syria?" Elie asked out of courtesy.

"Not yet. But a market may very well open up there soon. In the meantime we export live cattle to the Socialist countries and frozen meat to Portugal, Egypt, Israel . . ."

"Israel!" Elie interrupted. "You mean to say you sell meat to the Zionists, and not to the Fatherland?"

His voice had a convincing patriotic edge to it. So convincing, in fact, that El-Zaoumi was disconcerted.

"Let's not talk about business," he mumbled, trying to overcome his embarrassment. "After all, we've come here to enjoy ourselves, haven't we, Kamel?" .

"So be it, El-Zaoumi," Elie said, like a forgiving teaching catching his pupil in the act. "Come, let us join the others."

A man in a gray striped suit was relaxing in an armchair reading a newspaper called *The Clarion*.

El-Zaoumi spotted him and said to Elie, "I almost forgot, Kamel. We have a guest with us today. See that man holding the paper? That's Abdul Latif Hashan, the editor of *Arab World*."

"Oh!" Elie said in appreciation.

"Come, I'll introduce you."

They went over and Elie gave a slight bow.

"Sir, permit me to introduce Kamel Amin Tabet," El-Zaoumi said. "One of our most successful businessmen and a Syrian citizen who is proud of his country."

Abdul Latif rose and shook hands with him.

"My name's Abdul Latif Hashan, editor of the *Arab World*. I've heard a lot about you, Kamel. It's a pleasure to make your acquaintance."

"The pleasure is all mine, Abdul Latif," Elie replied.

El-Zaoumi pulled over two chairs and a lively conversation ensued.

At first they dwelt on politics, especially the tension resulting from the Soviet arms shipments to Cuba. The United States had convened an urgent meeting of the Organization of American States to denounce the regime in Havana. Arturo Frondizi, President of Argentina, was among the chief supporters of the proposal.

"I've heard the Americans have offered Argentina large-scale technical and financial aid to get them to support the Kennedy Doctrine," Hashan said.

"Yes, but that doesn't stop the people in the streets from yelling, *Cuba, si—Yankee, no*," Elie replied. "Only yesterday I saw a demonstration in front of the American Embassy in Buenos Aires."

"Nevertheless, I believe that in the end money will win out," Hashan said. "What is your opinion, Kamel?"

"Look here, Latif," Elie chided him. "I see you're no better than us merchants. You also think in terms of money."

Abdul Latif Hashan smiled and made no reply. There was a moment of tense silence, finally broken by El-Zaoumi.

"I think I'll have something to drink," he said, excusing himself.

Elie decided to touch on a subject closer to Hashan's heart.

"I've read your paper. I find it extremely interesting, though politically it's rather on the moderate side."

"What does a businessman like you, Kamel, want with politics?" Hashan said, attempting to sting him.

"In today's conditions, even politics is a business," Elie replied, and immediately added, "I believe that if the *Arab World* appeared in Damascus, they'd accuse you of pro-Western tendencies."

Hashan looked at him in confusion, then spread out his hands.

"Out of sight, out of mind," he said. "When one is far from home, one must adjust oneself to local customs."

"Since you've begun with proverbs," Elie said, "let me reply with one of my own: Once a Syrian—always a Syrian.

A citizen who loves his country keeps faith with it even when abroad."

"You're right, Kamel," Hashan apologized.

He looked at the man with the moustache opposite him and racked his brain. For the moment he could find no answer to the question that was bothering him. If Kamel Amin Tabet was such an ardent patriot, why was he here in Argentina? Why wasn't he in Syria trying to do something for his country's backward economy? Why did he prefer to do business in a foreign country?

He was about to ask the question, but then thought better of it. Elie's tongue was a bit too sharp for his liking.

This Kamel probably has an answer for that too, he said to himself, then added out loud, "Would you like to subscribe to my paper?"

"Very much," Elie replied, pulling out a checkbook for the Import-Export Bank in Buenos Aires.

"No!" Abdul Latif exclaimed. "I won't take money from you!"

"Why not, my brother?" Elie asked.

"I don't take money from friends."

"But if I insist?"

"Then I'll have to refuse."

"As you wish, dear Abdul Latif," Elie said, putting the checkbook back in his breast pocket.

"How can I thank you?"

Abdul Latif twirled his moustache and smiled. "By coming to the club more often. It's not every day that I find a conversation partner as sharp-witted as you."

Elie took full advantage of the invitation. He visited the club at least three evenings a week. His knowledge on a wide range of subjects gained him Abdul Hashan's admiration, and his friendship too, after he put a number of giant ads in his paper.

One evening, before leaving, Hashan turned to Elie and said, "tomorrow evening they're having an official reception at the embassy. The wife of the economic attache is having a birthday, and I have the honor to invite you."

The Syrian Embassy building is located in Avenida Viamonte, in the luxury section of the lower city. When the yellow taxi pulled up in front of the two-story building, all the windows were lit up and the racket inside told Elie that the celebration was already going full swing.

He got out, paid the driver, and went up to the big iron gate. A sentry in a natty uniform gave him a questioning look.

"Good evening, sir," the sentry said politely. "Have you been invited to the reception?"

Elie showed him the invitation.

The sentry nodded and opened the gate.

Inside there were about twenty couples, sipping cocktails and talking with some animation. Elie recognized some of the leaders of the Buenos Aires Arab community.

There were the First Secretary of the Egyptian Embassy and his wife, a well-known Syrian lawyer, and the manager of a local travel agency who organized trips to Syria. There were a few people there whom he couldn't identify, but he assumed they held key positions in the Syrian emigrant colonly of Buenos Aires.

Underneath a large wall painting he spotted his friend Abdul Latif Hashan, talking to a woman in a long black evening gown.

He went over.

"May I break in?" he asked politely.

"By all means." Hashan smiled. "Allow me to introduce Mr. Kamel Amin Tabet, one of our most talented men. Kamel, this is Madame Hamisa, the wife of our beloved attache."

Elie made a light bow in the best Oriental tradition and pressed her small hand. She raised a wan smile and inclined her head.

"May Allah grant you long years of happiness," Elie said ardently. "Your joy is the joy of us all."

She smiled more warmly.

"You're flattering me, Tabet. But I enjoy flattery."

"Thank you, Madame."

Elie went over to the refreshment table and took several hors d'oeuvres. A few minutes later, Hashan joined him.

"You made a great impression on the attache's wife," he told him. "She says that you're a very impressive man."

"I'm honored," said Elie.

A moment later Abdul Latif said, "Come, I'll introduce you to our military attache."

"You're going to too much trouble, Hashan," Elie mumbled.

"Oh, think nothing of it."

This officer with a pensive look and aquiline nose had

aroused Elie's curiosity. He was wearing a Syrian general's uniform with decorations and a white officer's hat with a black peak. Elie put his age in the early forties.

"General, allow me to introduce a man who's a Syrian patriot in every sense of the word," Hashan said emotionally. "Kamel Amin Tabet."

Elie Cohn took a polite look at the general and for some reason got the impression that he wasn't the talkative type.

His stolid unsmiling greeting testified that he didn't feel at home at a cocktail party and preferred to prove himself in deeds rather than words.

"Kamel, this is General Amin El-Hafez, the military attache of the embassy."

"It's a great honor for me to meet you personally, General," Elie murmured as he shook the attache's powerful bony hand.

El-Hafez was not the type for unnecessary demonstrations of friendship and quickly withdrew his hand.

I'll have to get in with him no matter what, Elie thought. It never hurts to have connections with a general.

From what he had learned about the Damascus regime, Elie knew that Syrian diplomatic representatives in foreign countries were people to respect.

Since the coup d'etat by Colonel Husni Zayim, in March, 1949, Syria had had no less than seven military take-overs, each providing scores of ambassadors, attaches, and advisors to Syrian embassies in every country of the world. Each military junta, on coming to power, took care to send the members of the deposed faction as far out of sight as possible, to prevent them from working against the party in power.

It was something of a vicious circle. Each group of leaders, on being toppled from power, would be sent to the diplomatic service abroad, and after a few years in exile would return and undermine the ruling regime in Damascus.

Something told Elie that sooner or later the silver-haired general would hit the headlines. Actually, it wasn't his idea alone. That morning, in a brief conversation with Avraham, his contact in Buenos Aires, he had been advised to make friends with the military attache at the Syrian Embassy and was even given some information about him.

Among other things, Elie had learned that the military attache was one of the leaders of the Baath party, a group that had begun working against the current regime in Damascus.

"I hear that in Syria there is unrest among the masses at present," he said.

"Yes, yes," El-Hafez mumbled. "Nasser has taken advantage of the union with us, and he's trying to take over. If it was up to me, I'd break that union."

"You believe Syria can make a go of it by herself?"

"I do indeed," El-Hafez said. "We have to replace the present regime. The Syrian Assembly is packed with bribed and corrupt representatives. I say this without reservations. They've been led astray by Nasser's phony slogans."

"But if I'm not mistaken, the Baath used to be in favor of the union, sir," Elie said, watching his interlocutor's expression change to one of surprise.

"The Baath?" he exclaimed. "What made you mention the Baath?"

Elie eyed him with genuine astonishment.

"Why, General, everyone's saying you're one of the leaders of the party that'll put an end to Syria's inferiority, and clear the atmosphere there."

Elie's words had hit the mark, and El-Hafez' face lit up. He still didn't believe that it was widely known that he was one of the active members of the party that had been driven underground by the Damascus regime, but the idea flattered him so much that he didn't take the trouble to ask Elie where he got his information.

"From your mouth to the ear of Allah, Kamel," he said enthusiastically. "Let's go up to my room, where we can talk quietly."

"With pleasure," Elie replied.

The first shot had been a bull's-eye. A compliment paid at the right time, he thought, had established him more firmly than the highest recommendations from the general's closest friends would have done.

El-Hafez's office on the second floor of the embassy building was simply furnished. The mahogany desk held a telephone, a framed picture of two smiling children, a number of papers, and a black leather case.

In one corner was a safe, which probably contained secret documents. Elie glanced at it and reflected how valuable it would be to get his hands on its contents.

In another corner stood a flowerpot with a prickly cactus. The remaining furniture consisted of a leather upholstered sofa and two broad armchairs facing the desk.

Elie sank into one of these and watched El-Hafez open a desk drawer and take out a whiskey bottle and two glasses. He poured himself a drink and offered one to his guest.

"You probably think I'm an infidel, Kamel." El-Hafez hastened to explain. "Maybe you weren't aware of it, but I'm not a Moslem. I belong to the Allawi faith, which allows us to drink as much as we wish. Now, Kamel my friend, would you care to join me?"

"Thanks, but I don't drink."

"So be it. To the Baath," he said, downing the drink in one gulp.

"To a free Syria," Elie added. "Incidentally, if I'm not mistaken, the Allawis are the oldest community in Syria, older even than the Druzes or the Moslems."

"You're right, Kamel," El-Hafez replied. "Our community has a long history. They say it goes all the way back to the time of the Canaanites. We've gone through periods of slaughter and uprisings. But there have also been better times, like during the French mandate in Syria. Then we had complete autonomy."

"And your religion allows you to drink hard liquor?" Elie continued on the same point.

"Oh, the Allawi religion is a very complicated business." El-Hafez chuckled. "Only a few old men in the community really know what it's all about. That may be the reason why the younger generation prefers to be secular in all respects. I'm no different. Tradition is for graybeards."

"But doesn't that prejudice the patriotic feelings that our Koran tries so diligently to inculcate?" Elie said, playing on a sensitive chord.

"Heaven forbid!" El-Hafez exclaimed. "Religion is one thing, and the State is something else. We're secular nationalists. We, that is the members of the Baath, want to bring progress to the entire Arab world. We're in favor of reforms and against all religious and personal interests."

"That sounds a bit like communism. Am I right?"

"Allah forbid!" the General exclaimed, and hastened to defend his party's principles.

"The theories of Karl Marx are based on materialism without human or spiritual values or a national conscience. Nations are nothing but large families, and the family of Arab nations cannot content itself with the ideas of Marx. And that's how we've developed the Baath outlook, which is socialism combined with nationalism and recognition of Man's creative spirit."

Elie Cohn knew that slogans were one thing and deeds another. The difference between a party's platform before and after it came to power is enormous. But he had no wish to argue with his host.

After all, the purpose of his visit was to make connections with the military attache, and what better way was there to gain an Arab's friendship than by letting him unburden himself?

Elie, who knew the party's history by heart, fashioned his questions to get El-Hafez to answer at length. He knew that as an active member in a party that had tried to seize power, El-Hafez was extremely sensitive in anything that regarded its status and glorious history.

"You claim the Baath will soon come to power, General," Elie said. "But as far as I know, your party hasn't been in existence very long and doesn't have many members."

"There you're wrong, my friend," El-Hafez hastened to correct him. "Actually, the Baath became a party in 1942, when Michel Aflak resigned from the teaching profession to become a propagandist. By 1947, the year the French left Syria, we had one thousand selected members."

"And how did he explain our defeat in Palestine in 1948?" Elie continued.

"Aflak claimed that we lost because of the social structure in the Arab states. He claimed, and justly, that a society based on disunity, dissension, and inequality prevents the Arabs from realizing their full potential."

"And what is the party's position at present?"

"At present we have 50,000 members distributed in eight-man cells throughout the Arab world. We could double the number, but we don't accept just anyone. We have to guard against adventurers, ne'er-do-wells, and enemy agents."

Elie took out a pack of cigarettes, offered one to El-Hafez, then lit up and took a long drag.

"Tell me, General," he said, "what are the chances of getting accepted as a regular member of the party?"

"Are you planning to go back to Syria in the near future?" El-Hafez asked.

Elie gave him a pensive look. Then he diverted his eyes to an imaginary point on the wall.

"You know, General, there are times when nostalgia gets

the better of you, and you have a hankering to see your homeland. You want to see the house where you lived, the streets where you played. To recall the wonderful days of childhood."

The general wasn't moved by Elie's sentimental confession. He remained cold and official as he said, "The party's constitution states that a member is accepted after a minimum of two years' candidacy, in which he has proved his sincerity and persistence, but since you are clearly an ardent patriot, you can take advantage of my friendship and save two years."

"I'm very grateful to you, General," Elie said and glanced at his watch. "It's getting late, I have to go."

He rose and shook El-Hafez' outstretched hand.

"I hope we'll meet again, General," he said.

"Of course. I'll remember you, Kamel."

6

Into the Lions' Den

Soon afterward, Elie Cohn left South America for the lions' den itself, where he could expect no help.

Before getting on the plane that would take him from Lod Airport to Munich, Germany, Elie met Zalman once again.

He received precise instructions regarding the next stage of his assignment.

"Your transmitter is with Zelinger in Munich. He'll give it to you along with the papers, in your new name. When you get to Damascus you'll be contacted by one of the employees of the Syrian Broadcasting Service—an emigrant like yourself —but don't put too much trust in him and don't try to locate him. It's his job to make contact with you."

"Any other instructions?" Elie asked.

"Yes, one more thing," Zalman said. "Good luck, Elie. Don't forget, we'll all be with you all the time you're in Syria. You'll never be alone."

"Are those Yitzhak's words?"

"No, it's what I say. After all, even in our department you're allowed to have a little personal initiative."

When the plane landed at Munich, Zelinger was already waiting at the airport.

"How do you feel, Elie?" he asked.

"Great. I'm dying to get down to work. I hate the tension that builds up before it actually starts."

Zelinger took out a pack of fragrant Cuban cigarillos, and offered one to Elie.

He declined politely.

"You've quit smoking just when things are starting to get hot?"

"I have to get used to it. As a Moslem I can't smoke too much and I can't drink."

"If that's how it is," Zelinger said, grinning, "then I'll permit myself to invite you to the tavern across the street. If they told me to stop smoking and drinking, I think I'd quit the Service. Apart from those pleasures what does a man have in this world?"

As they sat in a dark corner of a cafe near the airport, Zelinger gave Elie his final instructions.

"This case I have with me contains everything you need. You might say it's a very up-to-date and diversified espionage kit. You have paper containing the code in invisible ink, a transistor radio with a miniature transmitter, an electric shaver with a cord that can serve as an antenna, dynamite fingers concealed in a package of Yardley soap—and, oh, yes, cyanide pills, for suicide."

He waited to see Elie's reaction.

"I know," Elie said. "Suicide only when everything else fails."

Zelinger shut his eyes and nodded.

"It's better not to think about it. Right now we have to figure out how to get this stuff through the Syrian border, where they've got pretty touchy lately. The only chance is by way of Lebanon."

Zelinger was lost in thought for a moment. Then his eyes lit up as the idea took shape.

"Tomorrow you take the Air France flight to Rome. There you take the train to Genoa and buy a ticket for the *Astoria*, which sails for Beirut on January the fifth. On the boat you'll be contacted by a Syrian Arab, a globe-trotting merchant like yourself, and he'll take you across the border. He's done it before, and you can rely on him."

"But it's four days till the boat leaves," Elie noted.

"In Europe the days are short. Anyway, there are a lot of formal arrangements you have to make before you can travel safely. I think you may have to change your itinerary and fly to Zurich, where they'll fix you up with visas for Italy and Syria.

"The Argentine passport won't cause you any problems. Of course, then you'll be able to open a separate account in a Swiss bank. At the same time you'll get acquainted with the account you already have there. That way you'll know how much you can allow yourself.

"You needn't get excited about the amount. And if you need to use it, don't be afraid it'll diminish. Someone whom it's better you don't know will see that it never gets below a certain minimum level."

"Minimum level?"

"Yes, a level anybody would be proud of."

Elie said good-bye and walked over to the airport. There were planes leaving Munich for Zurich practically every hour of the day. He bought a ticket and took off.

Europe, for Elie, was only a means for getting to his destination. Unlike the elderly tourist couple across the aisle, he wasn't absorbed by the scenery. His thoughts were all concentrated on more important matters.

The *Astoria* was decidedly an economy-class boat. Most of the passengers were small businessmen, unimportant merchants. All of them were heading for Beirut or for Damascus via Beirut.

Elie felt like a fish in water. The language and customs were familiar to him. And he was welcomed by the captain, who had heard he was a wealthy and generous Damascus merchant. Nothing worried him except who his contact man would be.

Elie went up on the main deck, where he leaned over the railing and watched the waves breaking over the bow. Night descended on the sea in an exquisite sunset, and then the moon filled the sky and gave the world a romantic aura.

All at once, by the light of the moon, with the lights of Genoa twinkling in the distance, he noticed another figure standing beside him, leaning on the rail.

"Kamel?"

Elie nodded.

"Follow me," the man said.

Elie obeyed and went down with him to a cabin in first class.

"My name is Majd Sheikh El-Ard," the man said, shaking hands.

"Pleased to meet you. Kamel Amin Tabet," Elie answered politely.

"Do you smoke?"

"Sometimes."

"I have some excellent Egyptian cigarettes," the man said. Elie took one, sniffed it, and smiled in pleasure.

"I think you know all about me," he said.

"One can never know everything. I've been told to help you cross the Syrian border, and I'm doing it because I have no great liking for the people guarding the border, and especially the leaders of the army. Do you like them?"

"I don't know," Elie replied. "Maybe they'll be gone by the time we get there."

Majd slapped him on the shoulder.

"I think we'll get along fine. You understand, they paid me for this job, but I don't do everything for money. Sometimes I have my own ideas on certain subjects, and then I do as I please."

"Tell me more about yourself, Majd. I've heard you're a merchant and a man of action."

Majd lowered his eyes modestly.

"Let's not exaggerate. I've had a bit of a career, but nothing special. You see, in Damascus I'm known as a successful merchant. People are jealous of me. The government also, because they don't like independent forces much.

"During the war—the Second World War—I spent most of the time in Germany. I supplied merchandise and bought army equipment, and I did good business with all the bureaus of the Nazi government. I didn't have anything against them. I even admired them for the way they were solving the Jewish problem.

"Personally, I wouldn't hurt a soul—Jew or Arab. I think I'm an understanding man, and I don't have destructive instincts. My own wife is Jewish, and it's thanks to her I got my Syrian citizenship."

Elie nodded in sympathy.

"And after the war?"

"After the war it was a bit tough. You know, till things got organized, law and order suddenly take over and nobody likes business and adventure anymore. I realized too late that I'm the type of guy who's made to succeed in times of trouble—wars, uprisings, that sort of thing. That's why when the Korean War broke out, I tried to get over there through the UN, but it didn't come off.

"I went to Argentina and started doing business. I met a lot of my friends from the war there. They've got hundreds of agents in Argentina from every country, and if you know your way around you can do all right. That's how they came to me and asked me to help you get across the border."

"What happens if you get caught?" Elie asked.

Majd scratched his head and hesitated.

"I haven't thought about it. I've got something in my blood that makes me itch for adventure. I'm the sort of guy that lives for the present. What happens tomorrow, *insh'allah.*"

Elie was absorbed in Majd's story and didn't notice that his cigarette had gone out. When he pulled on it he found it cold. He crushed it in the ashtray and stretched.

"It's best we don't see much of each other before we get to Beirut," Majd said. "You can rely on me. I won't leave you till we arrive in Damascus."

The boat tied up at the wharf and the passengers started disembarking. On the front of the building a large canvas banner said: *Welcome to Beirut.*

Elie looked around. In the distance he could see the mountains and the buildings of the Paris of the Middle East. He made his way to the passenger hall, straightened his tie, and fingered the leather strap of his suitcase.

"Anything to declare?" the customs officer asked.

Elie smiled and looked at Majd.

"Why don't you tell him what we have in the suitcase?" he said.

Majd went over to the customs officer and whispered something in his ear. The latter gave Elie a knowing look and smiled.

"A hundred dollars will clear everything," Majd said.

Without hesitating, Elie pulled out a hundred-dollar bill and slipped it into the officer's hand.

He replied by making a rapid and large chalk mark on his luggage.

"You can get anything you want here," Majd said. "If you know how to invest. The Orient is dying for *baksheesh.*"

They both grinned.

"I'm going to call my driver. We'll use my car to get to the border," Majd said. Then he proceeded to the phone booth at the entrance to the port.

While they were waiting for the car, they went into the cafe near the pier and ordered a cold drink. Grave-looking men sat around and stolidly regarded the two merchants sipping tamarindi. Then they heard a horn honk outside, and Majd nodded to Elie that it was time to get going.

"The car's waiting, Kamel."

Elie left the bottle on the table.

The car left the harbor area, flashed by the bonded warehouses, and entered the city and the noise of the bustling streets.

Elie kept his eyes open and made a mental note of everything that he observed. For a moment he thought about the long way he had come, and smiled to himself in satisfaction.

"You seem to be enjoying Lebanon very much," Majd remarked, noting the expression on his face.

"I was thinking how easy it is to bribe the local customs officials."

Majd lit a cigarette.

"Oh, there's no easier life than that here in Lebanon. This is a very liberal Arab country. It lives off tourists, and it wouldn't think of putting difficulties in their way."

"But why didn't he look through my luggage? Maybe I'm carrying hashish. Maybe I've got a secret transmitter in that suitcase."

"Why should you want to do that, Kamel? I myself believe you're smuggling something in your luggage. Maybe hashish, maybe something like it. But I told the customs man you're carrying pornographic literature."

Elie smiled in satisfaction.

Majd was a shrewd operator who no doubt knew all there was to know about the art of smuggling.

The car carrying Sheikh Majd and Elie Cohn squealed to a stop in front of the barrier at the Syria-Lebanon border. In the trunk were Elie's suitcases, loaded with broadcasting equipment and other incriminating articles.

The inspection man who approached the car looked cheerful and expectant. The elegant limousine held a great many possibilities, he reckoned.

"Keep cool, Kamel," Majd said. "Let me handle him."

The Syrian security officer leaned on the window frame of the car and put out his hand for their papers.

They handed him their passports and entry visas. He made a quick comparison between the photos and the men's faces, then handed them back.

"Anything to declare?" he asked.

"You kidding, Abu-Heldon?" Sheikh Majd cried and burst out of the car with a cry of joy. "It's been a long time, old pal," he said, slapping the sentry on the shoulder.

For a moment the two of them stood embracing each other's necks, oriental style. Then Elie noticed they were conversing in whispers, and immediately afterward Sheikh Majd hurried back to the car.

"My dear friend Abu-Heldon." he said, "is in financial

troubles. Five hundred dollars would improve his situation a lot."

Cohn nodded, withdrew the money from his wallet, and passed it on to the security officer via Majd Then the gate was lifted and the limousine crossed the border into Syria.

As they drove away, Elie couldn't conceal his curiosity.

"Is Abu-Heldon," he asked, "a good friend of yours?"

"Abu-Heldon?" Majd laughed. "Why, that's a name I made up on the spur of the moment. His real name is Nasser ad-Din Waladi. We've met here a few times before."

7

Nazi-Hunting in Damascus

The bustling streets of Damascus were a picturesque place in which to be swallowed up. If Elie's mission had been to mix in with the crowd, there would have been nothing easier. However, his assignment was to be conspicuous from the first moment.

He spent his first days in Damascus in the Samara Hotel, until, through Sheikh Majd, he found an elegant villa in the Abu-Ramana quarter, which looked out on Syrian Army Headquarters and faced the entrance to a luxurious dwelling where the Syrian Government put up its official guests.

The same quarter also boasted the residence of the heads of the regime, the rich men of Damascus, and the diplomatic representatives of the various foreign legations.

Standing at the window and looking out on the wonderful scenery, Elie knew that no house anywhere else was worth the high rent of his villa.

When the landlord demanded a year's rent in advance, Elie didn't think twice. He thrust into his hand, in cash, thirteen hundred Syrian pounds.

The well-known Arab garrulity, he knew, would quickly spread the news about the affluent new resident, and people would soon be knocking at his door.

Elie's first days in Damascus removed the last trace of apprehension from his mind. Ensconced in his lordly villa, there was no better time to get in with the ruling circles.

A few months earlier the United Arab Republic had been dissolved, and the chief worry of the new heads of state was a possible counterrevolution inspired by Egypt. The business of espionage did not occupy their attention at all.

Elie Cohn and people like him were the kind most in demand by the ruling faction, which had recently taken over. He was an ardent patriot, well connected, and munificent.

Kamel Amin Tabet, the millionaire and successful business-man, was the right man in the right place.

There was no doubt—and Cohn was the first to admit it—
that the many letters of recommendation had opened the
doors of high society to him. His checkbook aroused respect
among the Damascus merchants and bankers—the very circles who had inspired and financed the revolution of September 29, 1961.

With ample funds at his disposal, Elie decided to play to
the hilt the role of an avowed Baathist and rich and generous
Syrian. At the same time, in the first phase he tried not to
commit himself entirely to the new regime. Tightrope walking
was a most important art in Syria at that time.

A few gestures of goodwill were enough to make all eyes
focus on him—especially the eyes of several rich merchants,
anxious to marry off their innocent daughters.

Elie declined all the offers of marriage that poured in, and
succeeded in remaining the most sought-after bachelor in Damascus.

One evening a tall, attractive man with silver hair and a
round face knocked on his door and introduced himself as the
Director of Foreign Broadcasting for Radio Damascus.

"Salem Saif!" Elie cried with feigned admiration. "I'm
happy to make your acquaintance."

Salem extended his hand for a warm shake.

"Have we met before?"

"No," Elie said, "but I've heard a lot about you, and I listened to your programs quite often when I was in Argentina."

"I'm happy to hear it," the man said modestly. "Incidentally, I assume you know precisely what brings me to you at
an hour like this?"

Elie nodded.

"Yes, I've heard there's some propaganda material for the
foreign broadcasts that I'm to look over."

"It may sound strange," Salem said, "but when I'm asked
to do something in exchange for something, I'm always ready
to comply with the request."

"I understand," Elie said, hastening to remove the slightest
trace of doubt. "I've been abroad many years, and I think I
know exactly what Syrian citizens want to hear when they're
away from their homeland."

Salem Saif bowed in capitulation.

"All the material will be placed at your disposal, Tabet. I
get it regularly from the Ministry of Information. In most

cases I have the final say regarding what gets broadcast. There is seldom need to censor my programs."

Elie knew that this was the man Zalman had told him about when he was in Israel. He also knew that the people who had recruited him had managed to give him the best possible story.

Saif, it later turned out, believed to the very last minute that Kamel Amin was nothing but an extremist Syrian patriot with certain political interests worth serving. Who knows, Saif thought to himself, if this man with the money and connections won't become the leader of the State, or at least cause a changeover in the leadership.

And so a warm friendship developed between Saif and Kamel, which expressed itself in exchanges of information and close cooperation in the excellent and important material supplied to Saif from the Syrian Ministry of Information.

Elie soon learned how to use this information for the purposes of his assignment, and every morning at a fixed hour and on a fixed frequency, he would transmit to Tel Aviv. His transmissions enjoyed complete protection: they were made from his home adjacent to the Headquarters of the Syrian Army, and were hidden among the thousands of transmissions being carried on the air.

To avoid the possibility of eavesdropping, Elie from time to time changed the frequency, as needed.

His connections with Salem Saif brought him to a tour of the radio station and later—as the result of a chance conversation—the idea was born of the "Emigrant's Hour," a program where Syrian emigrants were interviewed and told about themselves and their doings abroad.

The moderator of the special program was Kamel Amin Tabet, who suddenly showed extraordinary talent as a radio commentator.

The Israeli Intelligence Services, following Elie's activity in Damascus, began listening regularly to the program. Elie incorporated information in the program, without arousing even the slightest suspicion.

When he wanted to notify Headquarters in Tel Aviv that everything was going well, he would insert the last sentence from *Robinson Crusoe,* which he gave in French, and in inverted order.

Despite all the careful work, however, the information he passed on was sterile and unimportant.

One evening, as he was leaning over the transmitter, he received an urgent directive from Israel to make every attempt to locate the Nazi criminal Franz Raedemacher, who was hiding in Syria under the assumed name of John Rosalie.

"What happens when I find him?" he asked.

"You find a way to eliminate him."

Elie broke off the connection and took out a fragrant cigar from the box on the table. For a moment he wondered how he would locate Rosalie. Then he had an idea. He snuffed out the cigar, put on his coat, and left the house.

The weather outside bespoke the coming of winter. A cool wind swept the streets and the city was still. Elie walked quickly along the mosaic sidewalks of the city, passed the closed spice shop, and proceeded straight to Roamada Square.

The spice and novelty merchant was at home, wrapped in a warm lounging robe. He peered at Kamel standing on the threshold and then gave a coo of satisfaction and opened the door wide.

"Ahalen wa-Sahalen, ya Sheikh," Majd said in welcome.

Kamel went in and a pleasant smell of tobacco filled his nostrils.

"Winter is knocking at the gates of Damascus," Majd said. "Or maybe I'm getting old. But I feel the cold in my bones."

He poured Kamel a glass of steaming, aromatic coffee, and invited him to make himself comfortable.

"What brings you to my home at a time like this?" Majd asked him, after inserting the mouthpiece of his nargileh pipe between his fleshy lips.

Kamel scanned his "friend's" face and looked for the right moment to say what he had to say.

It's too early, he said to himself, to toss out the purpose of my visit without arousing suspicion. He decided to talk about anything at all before touching on the crucial point.

The box of fragrant Cuban cigars he had brought with him as a present gladdened the heart of his host. He put down the nargileh, chose a cigar, lit it, cleared his throat, and turned to Kamel.

"A fine cigar," he said. "Do you have many of these?"

"Well, I received a small shipment from Cuba for advertising purposes. I think I'll be ordering a much larger quantity. Do you think they'll go over here?"

"They'll go excellently, with the bigwigs."

He blew a bluish smoke ring. "Do you think you could get me some of these?"

"I'll do everything to see that they get here in time. Incidentally, the cigars reminded me of something. My agent in Argentina tells me he's been trying to locate the address of a friend of his, a German by the name of Rosalie. I was wondering if I could help him out. I've heard rumors that Rosalie is living in Damascus, maybe even under a different name."

"No, he's still here under his real name, from when he was Eichmann's friend in the Jewish Solution Department. As you can probably imagine, I have some dealings with the local Nazi colony and in Europe. I think I can show you where he lives."

Elie stretched.

"Oh, there's no rush, Majd. It can wait a day or two. The cigars will be arriving in any case."

"Kamel, you needn't hurt my feelings. I'm not doing this for the sake of the cigars. Come, we'll go there now. Rosalie's always home at this hour."

Majd got up, removed his lounging robe, and put on a black suit jacket.

"Come, I'll drive you over," he offered. "Maybe I'll even go in and introduce you."

Elie tried to dissuade him.

"Don't go to too much trouble, Majd. The weather outside isn't the best thing for your bones, remember?"

"Well, at least I'll show you the place and come back."

Elie didn't put up any more resistance.

The black limousine in the garage started smoothly and Majd's driver lightly guided it through the peaceful streets of Damascus. In the evening silence the whirr of the engine was clearly audible.

A few minutes later the car pulled up beside the bridge opposite the Central Bank.

Majd pointed out the house.

"The Rosalies live on the fourth floor."

Rays of light penetrated through the shuttered windows. Someone was at home.

"What's the name of the street?"

"Shahabander. It's the third building from the Central Bank. If you like we can check the house number."

Elie raised his hand to stop him.

"There's no need. The postman probably knows the family. At least from the well-kept garden."

"Rosalie is a kind of meticulous German." Majd chuckled.

"You know how the Germans are. They love precision. You can smell them a mile away."

Elie stretched.

"Well, that's it for tonight. I'm glad I've managed to help Sepalio a bit."

"Sepalio?"

"My agent in Argentina."

That evening, after saying good-bye to Majd, Elie made his way on foot to the El-Sharq nightclub on the south side of the city.

The El-Sharq was a gathering place for shady businessmen and their hangers-on. The atmosphere was dim and intimate. Only a few reddish lights flickered in the gloom, and not many more than that on the bandstand. Smoke from cigarettes and nargilehs filled the room.

A man in a turban greeted Elie with an oriental bow and an ear-to-ear smile.

Elie slipped him a pound note and asked, "Is Springer here?"

The man nodded.

"If you ask me, I don't know when he isn't here. I think he's chasing after Samil the dancer."

Elie smiled and went inside.

A big-bellied waiter led him to a table in the middle of the room, and in return for baksheesh, agreed to send Springer over.

"Tell him a good friend of Sheikh Al-Ard wants to see him," Elie whispered in the waiter's ear, and he was gone in the wink of an eye.

Meanwhile the lights dimmed and a colored spotlight illuminated the area in the middle of the hall.

The sound of ouds and drums filled the air until suddenly Samil appeared from behind the curtains, wearing muslin veils, her midriff bare.

She started gyrating, then faster and faster, bumping and grinding.

A broad-shouldered man with puffy white skin tapped Elie's arm. "Good evening."

"Sit down, Mr. Springer," Elie said without any preamble.

"With whom do I have the pleasure?"

"With Mr. Thousand Dollars."

The man gulped.

"What do I have to do, Mr. Thousand Dollars?"

"Do you know a man by the name of Raedemacher?"

Springer scratched his face.

"Is that one of the Nazi colony here in Damascus?"

The waiter brought their drinks, and Elie motioned to him to bring another round.

"You're only partly right," he said. "The man was a Nazi but now he's a worn-out one. Nevertheless, he is dangerous to the regime. He lives on Shahabander Street, not far from the Central Bank Building, under the name of John Rosalie."

Springer grinned broadly.

"Why didn't you say it was that son of a bitch?"

Elie rolled his glass between his fingers.

"A thousand dollars to put him out of the way."

"A thousand dollars for a dangerous job like that?"

"That's what the party is prepared to allot for the purpose —in addition, of course, to turning a blind eye to the shady deals you conduct here."

Springer nodded.

"I understand. You can leave it to me."

Elie pulled out a role of banknotes and gave him the money.

"Remember!" he warned. "Rosalie for that money, or your business here comes to an end."

Samil approached their table, continuing to roll her hips furiously. Her body twisted and quivered and tiny droplets of sweat covered her torso.

"Beautiful, isn't she?" Springer said.

"Depraved," Elie declared like a decent Moslem, and walked out.

He had the distinct feeling that the mission would be accomplished.

The next day Elie was invited to honor with his presence a party thrown by Salem Saif.

"Among the guests," Salem whispered as if revealing a secret, "Will be all the Who's Who of our top brass."

"You sure they'll all be there?" Elie asked.

"Up to now they've never disappointed me. My parties aren't modest but they're not formal either. Army men like to be informal after working hours. Tell me, Kamel, can I count on you?"

"You're doing too much for me, Saif," Elie said. "I'll have to pay you back soon with a string of parties."

Saif stretched out his hands in a gesture of respect. "May it be for your good health, Amin."

8

Entertaining the Syrian
Top Brass

Salem Saif's apartment was located in a luxury quarter. It had four elaborately appointed rooms, two of which served as salons.

A cocktail party in Salem's apartment, it later turned out, was more than an important social event; decisions on matters of state were sometimes made there and quarrels broke out at these gatherings of the Syrian brass.

As a swarthy servant was taking his coat, a dignified woman swept out of the first salon and extended her hand to Elie.

"Good evening, Kamel," she said, as if they had known each other for ages. "You honor our gathering with your presence."

She was a well-built redhead packed into a striped evening gown that emphasized her outstanding feminine charms. Her face was coated with a thick layer of makeup that hid her real age.

"I'm glad that you're happy to see me," Elie said. "Nevertheless, I'd be pleased to make the acquaintance of Milady, who apparently knows me from somewhere," he said very courteously.

"My name is Kamila Saif. I'm Salem's sister-in-law."

"Ah, yes. Am I early?"

"No, not especially. A number of guests are already here. Come, I'll introduce you to some people who are anxious to meet you."

She took Elie's hand and led him to a big parlor. Though most of the guests in the room were in dress uniform, others wore dark business suits. Even at first glance Elie could tell that most of them were tipsy.

"Wait here a minute, Kamel," his hostess said. "There's a young colonel who'd like to meet you."

She disappeared and for a moment was swallowed up among the guests. When she came back, she had a young officer in tow.

He extended his hand.

"Pleased to meet you, Mr. Tabet," he said. "My name's Colonel Salim Khatoum."

"I have to receive the other guests till my brother-in-law gets here. Pardon me if I leave you two alone," Kamila said, and left with a polite curtsy.

"Haven't we met before?" the officer asked suddenly.

"I don't believe so. I'm an emigrant from Argentina. Here only a few months," Cohn said.

"Nevertheless, you've managed to make quite a reputation as a philanthropist and successful merchant, and the entire elite is talking about the patriot Amin Tabet," the officer said with unconcealed admiration. "How do you explain your success?"

Elie cleared his throat.

"It's clear that on an army salary and with frequent coups d'etat you can't get very far. As the son of parents from Haleb who emigrated to Egypt and the Argentina, I managed to pull off a few good deals and collect a bit of money. And you know how it is." Elie winked to the officer. "Money always comes to money. And honor comes running after."

Khatoum looked at him wide-eyed, and his teeth glittered under his large moustache.

"Revolutions are essential for a regime that hasn't yet fixed its course," he said. "Syria is still dancing to Nasser's tune, and only a stable and firm regime can bring about the transformation that'll make Syria independent and the leader of the Arab world. Nasser is too soft on the West and imperialism. He's betraying the Arab cause."

"But who can guarantee that the new regime will grant Syria this security?" Cohn asked.

"No one can guarantee it. But we mustn't stop trying. The Baath began as a small party. Now it's a tremendous force. Isn't that how the Communist movement started? Isn't that how the Cuban revolution began?"

"Of course," Elie said. "And what happens if the officers' corps starts a new movement that overthrows the Baath?"

"Such a movement cannot arise," Khatoum said positively. "But if it does arise and its principles are just and its power great, the entire army will likely follow it."

"You too?"

"I'm an army man. I carry out orders," Salim said proudly. "An army man shouldn't mix in politics. His job is to fight."

He sighed briefly.

"It's a great sport, if you want my personal opinion."
Elie downed the last of the drink.

"The day after tomorrow I'm having a little party at my place, with lots of girls and drinks. Would you honor me with your presence, Colonel?"

Khatoum was obviously flattered.

"I'll try to be there," he said, "and I hope there'll be lots of action."

By the end of the party that evening, Elie had precise information on the Baath's plans for a military take-over. He returned home, waited for the morning transmission hour, and passed the information on to Tel Aviv.

"Nice work. Everything proceeding as anticipated," came the answer from Headquarters.

For the party at his home the next evening, Elie recruited the help of two of his close friends. He gave them the key to the apartment and told them to make all the arrangements. He preferred to go out and invite his close friends personally.

Access to them, even in the top-secret offices, was no problem. Kamel Amin Tabet was the only man permitted to circulate freely in the corridors of Syrian Army Headquarters.

On the evening of the party a number of agreeable girls were recruited from the Syrian Defense Ministry to serve as hostesses to the officers and top leadership, all under the guise of a birthday party.

The guests arrived one after the other, stretched out on the carpet and enjoyed being out of the limelight. The intimate atmosphere, lit only by flickering candles, was perfect; the selected guests were delighted.

The bar included all the local and imported wines and liquors. Kamel Amin Tabet wasn't miserly about the food and drink served in his house.

About ten o'clock Salim Khatoum appeared, somewhat tired and apparently worried.

"You look as though you need entertainment in the worst way," said Elie, greeting him with a smile. "But first wash away the dust of the road."

"You take care of everybody down to the last detail," Salim remarked.

"That's how I make friends and influence people."

"I'll remember that formula," Salim said and went into the bathroom.

"You can use the robe hanging in the closet," Elie called after him. "Feel right at home."

Salim's mood improved. He stripped off his uniform, donned the robe, and sat down in comfort. The robe was airy and comfortable.

"Tell me, Kamel, what's in store for us this evening?"

"I've invited a few close friends and we're having a small party. Officially it's a birthday party. But just between the two of us—" he winked—"it's to celebrate the successful conclusion of a big deal."

A stunning girl in a short skirt filled their glasses that stood on a low taboret. Salim couldn't take his eyes off her. It seemed that Kamel had shown great consideration for Salim's desires.

He invited the girl to come and pour them another drink.

"I feel I could drink a whole barrelful," Salim said.

"Even if I do the pouring?" Elie asked slyly.

Salim laughed. "I doubt if there's another host like you in all Damascus," he said. "Argentina taught you a lot about hospitality."

Elie rejected all this with both hands.

"I didn't need Argentina to learn hospitality. My whole family has always enjoyed giving parties. But traveling to other countries taught me new ways to please my guests— made me a sort of international *bon vivant*."

Salim nodded.

"In any case, I certainly enjoy being here. Especially after all the long days of boredom there on the Palestine border in those bunkers and tunnels we built to defend against an Israeli air attack."

Salim straightened up. "Did you know that the border is full of subterranean passageways inhabited by hundreds of Syrian soldiers?"

Elie raised his eyebrows. "Really?"

"You see, it's kind of an underground Maginot Line. It allows you to look out on the Israeli border and see the whole countryside. Remind me sometime, Kamel, and I'll take you on a tour of the place."

"Are you authorized to do that?" Elie asked suspiciously.

"Why not? I'm the regional commander there," Salim said proudly.

"But I'm only a loyal citizen," Elie explained.

"Don't worry, my friend. You're close to the regime. You're one of us."

Elie smiled to himself.

"Come, Salim, let's forget politics, and celebrate the evening with wine and women."

"Of course," Salim said. "Let's give the girls a good time."

Elie got up and intimated to the girl serving the drinks to make the Colonel feel at home.

"Let him get all his troubles off his chest. But if you hear something suspicious, don't forget to tell me about it."

She curtsied humbly and went over to the Colonel.

"Good evening, Colonel," she said.

"Good evening, beautiful." He moved over to make room for her. "Sit down beside me. I don't want to be alone this evening."

She sat down.

"Kamel asked me to make you feel at home," she murmured, "but not what you're expecting."

"I don't understand," he said.

"I'm a good friend of Kamel's, and I trust him. He asked me to come to his birthday party. He told me there'd be many important people, army officers, and intellectuals." She gave him a long look. "That's why I agreed to come."

Salim chuckled out loud.

"Okay, innocence." He laughed. "But hospitality demands at least a little kiss."

She drew back slightly. Then she understood she had no choice.

"Just one," she said in a low voice. "But don't ask me to go too far. I'm not in the habit of doing that, and especially not with a man I don't know, and in such a crowd."

"Don't worry about it. It'll be okay."

The girl knelt down beside Salim's knees, leaned forward, and kissed him on the cheek.

"That's no good," Salim protested. "You know I meant a kiss on the lips."

The girl hesitated a moment, as if this was the first time she was doing this with a man. Then her body pressed forward. Her lips attached themselves to Salim's lustily.

Salim wasn't ready to give up. He had been promised a girl who would make his stay agreeable.

"Didn't they tell you what your job was?" he asked.

She lowered her gaze shyly and blinked.

"I'm a typist in the Defense Ministry. I'm not the kind of girl you think, Colonel."

Salim opened his eyes wide and looked her body over with interest.

"The Defense Ministry, and a sharp-looking chick like you?" he murmured in amazement. "What's going on in this country these days?"

"Is that so surprising, Salim?" she asked. "Can't a girl like me work there?"

He nodded. "Why not? In fact, it's a very nice idea. I think the heads of our Ministry have learned that trick from the West. Beautiful girls in the Security Service."

His hand slid down her back and embraced her hips. She tried to get away but he hugged her tight. "How about a little cooperation between the Defense Ministry and the Army, or are your services only for civilians?"

She drew back and Salim smiled. Beside him in the half-lit room was another colonel.

"Tell me, Colonel," Salim said to him, "why don't they try to develop friendly relations between the Defense Ministry and the Army."

"You're drunk, sir. Anyway, what is the Defense Ministry if not the planning head of the executive arm?"

"If so, why does a cute little typist from the Defense Ministry try to get away from an army officer?"

The colonel smiled to himself.

"Tell her she fascinates you. Tell her about your army adventures. Your many connections, if you have any. Those girls love to hear secrets from a military man—it gives them a feeling of self-importance. When they're convinced that you trust them, they give in just like that."

Salim opened his eyes wide.

"But why should I give away security secrets to a girl I hardly know?"

The colonel shrugged.

"What are you worried about? She's a senior employee of the Defense Ministry."

Salim smiled.

"You sure it'll work?"

"It has to work. My own girl loves to hear about my military adventures. She asks to hear more and more. In that field you can rely on them."

"And what if they're setting a trap for me?"

"Trap?" The colonel smiled. "In the home of Kamel Tabet?"

Salim scratched his head. "You're probably right. I'll have to try it."

The next day an army messenger knocked on Kamel's door with a telegram from Ma'azi Zaher a-Din, commander of the army camp at El-Hama on the Israeli border:

On the recommendation of Salim Khatoum (the cable read) *and for the sake of our friendship, allow me to invite you on a courtesy tour of our base.*

The army courier produced an application form and transit permits to be signed.

Later the same day a military command car pulled up and took Elie to the Syrian-Israeli border.

Elie arrived at the entrance of the most important base on the Israeli border, and the gates opened without any difficulty. A sergeant volunteered to take him to the headquarters of Ma'azi Zaher a-Din.

"We'll continue afterward, gentlemen," Ma'azi Zaher a-Din told his deputies when he spotted Kamel.

He extended his hand.

"I'm happy you've decided to visit us," he said. Come and I'll show you a few things that no doubt will gladden the heart of a Syrian patriot."

They left the command room and climbed a small hill, overlooking the fields of Kibbutz Tel-Katsir and Lake Kinneret.

"From here Israel looks like a beautiful carpet on the map," Ma'azi Zaher a-Din said. "All green and cultivated."

He cleared his throat. "If this area was in our hands, Syria would have living space, access to the sea, and an excellent means of pressuring Nasser, Hussein, and all the rest."

Elie looked at the officer and his eyes held a perplexed expression.

"If so, with all the armaments we have and with this excellent position, why can't we drive them into the sea?"

"If it were only up to us, I assure you that the Israelis would have been gone long ago. The trouble is that the Israelis have world sympathy, and the big wheels are protecting this little bastard nation."

"What about the Israeli army?" Elie asked carefully.

Ma'azi Zaher a-Din made a face.

"Yes, they have an army that any Arab country would be proud of. But as you will understand, that isn't what's stopping us."

"Then what is?"

"Look, Kamel. We have better armaments than they have. We have several times more men. We have topographic superiority. But all this isn't enough in modern warfare. What we're lacking is the support of public opinion and the power to fight the entire West—which is behind Israel."

"Then why do the authorities proclaim war against the Jews morning and night?"

"It's probably good for politics. But just between us, I may tell you that it's very bad for the army."

Elie took the binoculars from the officer and again looked out over the plain at the foot of the ridge.

The lenses of the binoculars enlarged the view ten times and more. Elie had no trouble making out the kibbutz workers below them, and the bare-legged girl kibbutzniks.

"What do you think about those bare Israeli girls?" Ma'azi Zaher a-Din asked him, after directing his own binoculars toward the spot where Elie was looking.

Elie spat on the ground.

"Disgusting!" he said, like a good Moslem who doesn't tolerate female nakedness in public.

The next morning, at the appointed hour, Elie transmitted to Tel Aviv an exact description of what he had seen on his visit to the Syrian border. The answer came back: "Try to make another trip through the area. We lack material on the third sector."

Another invitation wasn't long in coming.

Elie became a close friend of the unit commander in the area and the only civilian permitted to circulate almost without restriction along Syria's strongest line of fortifications— that on the great ridge.

The defense plans, the concentrated armaments, the fortifications, the attack plans, and facts and figures about the strength of the force, were revealed to Elie Cohn through the courtesy of his good friends, the local commanders.

In exchange, Elie gave them presents and entertained them in his home at all hours.

After his second visit to the site, Elie thanked his kind host and told him that from then on—as a sign of true friendship —he was free to come and go in his home as he pleased.

"You've given me the feeling that you trust me," Elie said. "I would like to return the compliment. I want you to know that my home is open to you any time you wish to come."

Ma'azi Zaher a-Din smiled pleasantly.

"And if you want to be entertained in suitable company," Elie added, "don't hesitate. Just let me know a day ahead of time, and everything'll be fine. You'll never lack wine, women, and diversion in the home of Kamel Amin Tabet."

The officer shook his hand warmly.

"Thanks," he said. "I always knew I could rely on you."

Zaher a-Din wasn't the type to scoff at such a hearty invitation, especially from an important person like Kamel Amin Tabet.

One morning, shortly after their meeting on the Israeli border, Zaher a-Din surprised his friend by dropping in for a visit at an unusually early hour. At that moment Elie was broadcasting to Israel on the transmitter in his bedroom. The rhythmic ringing of the doorbell revealed the caller's identity.

Elie wasn't at a loss. He quickly broke off contact, replaced the cover on the transmitter, and went to open the door.

"Welcome," he cried, and fell into his friend's arms. "What brings you at such an hour?"

"I took a special furlough to fix up a few things in Damascus and I said to myself that it's time to meet the Defense Secretary, maybe I'll drop in and have a cup of coffee."

Elie bowed humbly.

"Always at your service, Ma'azi," he said.

Zaher a-Din passed through the house and made straight for the bedroom, where he flopped on the innerspring bed.

"My dear friend, it's great to be here," he sighed, and stretched out.

Elie hurried to the room, shaking almost uncontrollably. On the dresser near the bed a few code papers were lying here and there.

"What's that?" Zahr a-Din asked, pointing to the papers.

Elie shrugged, and without blinking an eyelash said, "It's a lousy crossword puzzle."

Though he hadn't been in Syria a year, Elie Cohn had already become a central figure, looked up to by masses of people. On the Syrian political horizon radical changes were shaping up. They called for background explanations and comprehensive information about all the men involved in the forthcoming revolution. Tel Aviv needed information, but

Elie couldn't transmit all of it fast enough with his small instrument.

Thus, one evening he got a message, "Pack up. Come to us."

The next day he informed his many friends and acquaintances that he had to go abroad for a while to arrange his affairs. To his closest friends he revealed his destination—Argentina.

There, in a rented suite in the Hotel Saitch, Elie again met with local emigrants, on business as it were. He established friendly contacts with them and with the men of the Argentine branch of Headquarters.

A few days later he left for Europe by KLM, and there in the dead of night with his hair dyed gray, he slipped onto an Olympic flight bound for Lod.

Zalman was waiting for him at the entrance to the airport in the small hours of the morning.

"I'm happy to see you again, Elie," he said, beaming. "You're looking great."

"Yes, this job is something like a vacation. At least as long as I keep out of prison."

They got into a car which drove them from the airport to Headquarters in Tel Aviv.

"Yitzhak," Zalman said, "is waiting for you on pins and needles. He's dying to have a look at Our Man in Damascus."

Elie signaled to him to lower his voice so the driver wouldn't overhear, but Zalman brushed him away.

"It's time you met some of our personnel here in Tel Aviv." So saying, he introduced the driver, an active member of the Security Service.

"I've been away a few months and you've turned the country into a police state, huh?" Elie chuckled.

"The chief," Zalman said with feigned anger, "wouldn't like to hear you talk like that."

After a hearty reception, accompanied by the clinking of glasses, Yitzhak and two of his colleagues sat and listened tensely to Elie's complete story.

Several hours later, after the entire picture had been unrolled, Yitzhak looked up and regarded his colleague in the service.

"It sounds fantastic even to an old fox like me."

"When I recommended Elie, I knew I was doing something for my pay," one of the men said.

Elie looked at him, but couldn't remember if he had ever run into him.

"That's enough for this evening," Yitzhak said. "Go home. They're liable to get worried."

"They can't be," Elie said. "I never even told them I was coming."

"You want to call them?"

"You do it, okay? I'm going to start moving."

"Okay, Kamel." Yitzhak smiled. "And don't forget to be here tomorrow at three."

"At three?"

Yitzhak nodded.

"Don't forget you have a family, boy. They won't let you slip out of their hands so easily."

The secretary spoke on the intercom.

"Chief," she said. "Someone from the family's on line two."

"Go home, Elie. I'll tell them you're on your way."

"Can I get a lift with our man from the airport?"

"Of course. Why do you think we got him out of bed at this hour?"

As the meeting broke up, they all rose and began to leave.

"While you were away, we received a number of pieces of equipment that are likely to help you in your work there," Yitzhak said. "A few offbeat cameras for copying documents. One of them is the size of a piece of chocolate, and the microfilm can easily be hidden in chess pieces or dice.

"The boxes, with the playing pieces, can be sent to your agent in Argentina, from where they'll be forwarded to Israel by diplomatic mail. It's extremely easy to use this little camera. I think you'll be able to double or triple the amount of material in this way, especially material that can stand a delay of at least a week."

"In other words, situation evaluations besides pure information," Elie said.

Yitzhak nodded.

"Yes. Detailed situation reports. At this moment we need a full estimate of the strength of the Baath. It seems that party would be the ruin of Israel."

"I guess so. It holds the key positions in the military command, and its rise to power is only a question of time."

"Do you think any of your friends is likely to replace the Syrian President tomorrow?"

"I don't like to make predictions. But El-Hafez seems to me the man who'll probably head the new leadership, and he'll probably take the job for himself."

9

Elie's Friend Becomes President of Syria

On March 8, 1963, shortly after Elie Cohn returned from a business trip in Europe and Argentina, the revolution took place as expected.

Curfew was imposed on Damascus. Tanks and troops filled the streets. Radio Damascus started playing marching tunes and Amin El-Hafez took his place behind the microphone and made a blood-and-thunder speech denouncing the Egyptian leadership and praising the Baath. The best friends of Kamel Amin Tabet became ministers and government leaders. El-Hafez himself, after a small palace revolt, was named President of the State.

From then on, Kamel's path was strewn with roses.

In honor of the revolution a magnificent party was thrown for all the supporters of the new regime. And who was the man behind it all? None other than Kamel Amin Tabet.

Expensive cars beside army vehicles, dress uniforms beside evening suits—that was the general picture at the splendid party held at Elie Cohn's villa in Damascus. The friendly, government-backed host shook hands with all the Who's Who of Syria, clinked glasses to the Party and the nation, and backslapped with friends from the good old days.

Among the guests could be seen the ministers of Information, Economy, and the Interior; generals and colonels such as Rabah Tawil, Zaher a-Din, Salim Khatoum, General Mahmoud Jaber, the Defense Minister, and many others.

General El-Hafez, the man on whose behalf the colonels had made the quiet revolution, showed up with his wife a bit later than usual. He was wearing an elegant black suit and his wife had on a mink stole, given to her by Elie.

Mrs. El-Hafez, like other women in the top leadership who had received presents from gentleman and benefactor Tabet, knew how to appreciate and repay his generosity. From women such as these Elie extracted an abundance of information about their husbands' activities.

That evening, however, Elie devoted most of his attention to Ibn-Ladan, whom Salim Khatoum had introduced as the man in charge of the Jordan River deviation project.

Elie shook his hand warmly.

"I'm willing to wager, sir, you are not a scion of the Syrian nation."

Ibn-Ladan smiled.

"Right, I come from Saudi Arabia. I'm a public works contractor and an engineer in my spare time."

"I've heard that you're about to alter the natural course of the Banias and divert it into Syria."

"Of course. It's a highly important project for Syria and the entire Arab world. Have you thought of a better way to liquidate an entire country without really trying?"

"You mean it can be done by diverting the waters of the Jordan?" Elie said in amazement.

"Of course. So long as they don't interfere with us."

"Who's likely to interfere?" Elie wondered.

"The Israelis, of course. They're using every means at their command. But we're designing a construction method that'll be safe even from air attacks."

"It's probably raised the cost, though."

"A bit, perhaps; but in the long run it'll be more efficient."

Elie pretended he didn't understand.

"The thing is we've introduced certain bombproof construction elements. Only a direct hit is likely to interfere with the work."

"What makes you think the Israelis are likely to use only aerial bombing?"

"That's the only possibility. It would be stupid to send a sabotage squad. The entire area is mined and they wouldn't get very far. So the only possibility is from the air."

"It's too bad I'm not in a business mood, Ibn-Ladan. I'd probably donate something to the cause if I knew exactly how those structures are supposed to help."

"Why, you can talk to the man in charge of it, in the Defense Ministry. He'll no doubt give you a thorough explanation. If necessary you can visit the site and see for yourself."

"Thank you," Elie said and bowed courteously. "I'll try to interest the Defense Minister."

From the subject of the Jordan deviation, Elie Cohn proceeded to talk about security on the Israeli border, the internal situation, and economic problems.

Talk flowed freely without anyone hesitating to reveal what he knew. The Baath and its leaders needed people like Elie Cohn. Especially his connections and money. If up to then it had been Elie who had courted the regime, now the tables were turned.

"Try to use your influence on our people abroad," El-Hafez' deputy suggested to him. "We need capital to consolidate our economy here in Syria."

"Allow me to interrupt, sir," Elie said meekly. "When people pour private capital into a country, especially in good dollars, they have the right to ask what it's being used for. Do you think you'll be able to tell every investor what his investment is being used for?"

"Apart from security matters," the aide said, "I assume we'll be able to do that."

"And what if it's decided that the lion's share of the money is to go for defense?"

"Perhaps we'd better set up a division to handle foreign investments. More or less detailed information on the investments will be given into the hands of a trustee, who'll find the way to get others to contribute."

"The question is, whom can we rely on?"

The man wrinkled his forehead in thought, then looked at Elie and asked, "Will you accept the job?"

Elie eyed him with feigned astonishment.

"Don't you think the decision is a bit hasty?"

The deputy brushed away his objections.

"I have the authority to say the last word in this matter," he said. "You can get to work."

A few days later, Elie began broadcasting to Israel frequently. His broadcasts were more effective. The information in them was of great value. Operation orders, decisions of the ruling party, armament plans, and topographic sketches of sensitive areas began to flow.

Some of them were given on the radio the next day—sometimes even before they were known to the Syrian leadership themselves.

The reports included all movements of the Syrian army, the dates of receipt of weapons, and the effectiveness of the equipment and its operational possibilities within the framework of the Syrian army.

The information was transmitted to Israel by every possible

means, and was utilized to the full. Later on, when he renewed the parties at his home, he chose suitable girls and, without arousing their suspicions, managed to persuade them to collect any information of value.

At the height of his wildest parties, he didn't hesitate to take series of pictures that would serve as first-rate extortion material.

A high-ranking French personage who attended one of these parties later said that the place, the people, and the scene resembled an oriental version of the *Ballet of Roses* or an orgy a la Christine Keeler.

Despite all his attempts at blackmail for security purposes, Cohn did nothing to soil his name. People who tried to take advantage of their connections with Elie in order to do business with the government were rejected by him with disgust.

"As a revolutionary man loyal to the Baath," he would burst out, "how do you expect to buy my heart with hush-money? Baksheesh went out with the advent of the Baath."

His patriotic pronouncements and unqualified loyalty to the regime raised Elie to hitherto unknown heights in the militaristic state. His civil standing reached a record high, and the proof of it came during the visit to Syria of General Ali Amer, Chief of the United Arab Command.

Elie Cohn was the only civilian who joined the tour of colonels and generals along the Israel-Syria border. He followed the explanations of the area given by the commander, and remembered all that could be remembered.

The military correspondents and photographers gave full coverage to the tour. Cameras flashed without letup. Had he wanted to, Elie Cohn could have avoided the camera lenses. No one would have noticed it. But he tried to push into the front lines and stand shoulder to shoulder with Amer.

The pictures were important to him for self-promotion among the high command.

Not long after the visit of Ali Amer, Elie was assigned an important mission. El-Hafez requested him to go on a reconciliation mission to the former president of Syria, Sallah al-Bitar, who was on convalescent leave in Jericho.

Elie set out, met with the elderly president, and had long talks with him about the principles of the Baath, doing all he could to persuade him to return and recognize the new regime.

"The Syrian nation appreciates your resourcefulness and admires your personality. We would like to see you among us."

"But I do not recognize the present regime," the old leader replied. "And the regime doesn't recognize me."

"The regime *does* recognize you. Though not the way you ran the country before the Baath came to power."

"If I understand your intentions, my return will symbolize my recognition of the regime, and that will be a considerable contribution to the party."

"Think about it, old man. There's no sense running away from reality," Elie counseled.

The talks continued for three more days. In the end, Sallah al-Bitar agreed to consider the proposal carefully. Elie took leave of him and returned to Damascus.

"El-Hafez," he was told on his arrival in Syria, "has had a bad kidney attack. He has to make an urgent trip to Paris for an operation."

"Can't I see him in his office?" Elie asked the President's secretary.

"I'm afraid not. He's been ordered to have a complete rest. But if it's urgent, you can join him on his way to the airport. He's leaving for Paris this afternoon."

"Tell him that's what I'll do."

On their way to the airport, Cohn revealed the development of his talks with Sallah al-Bitar, hinting that it was likely that the elderly leader would agree to return to Damascus. But without fanfare.

"The old boy's starting to soften," El-Hafez chuckled to himself.

"He's still as tough as a cedar of Lebanon," Cohn said.

"No. He softened the moment he agreed to receive you at his home in Jericho," El-Hafez explained. "He knew very well that you were my personal envoy. And recognition of your mission is recognition of me."

He sighed and clasped his hips, which had contracted in a momentary convulsion.

"When I come back well from Paris, I'll begin reorganizing things. That old man is likely to raise the Baath's standing among the masses, especially the opponents of the regime."

Elie shook El-Hafez' hand before he got on the plane, and wished him a quick recovery. Then the plane took off and disappeared in the bluish horizon.

A short while later, Tel Aviv knew that El-Hafez had left for an urgent kidney operation in Paris.

"The recovery is likely to take three weeks. In your opinion, are the opponents of the regime strong enough to make a counterrevolution in that time?" asked a message from Tel Aviv.

Elie grinned.

"As a Baath man," he coded back, "I don't believe so. All the opponents are behind bars."

He broke off the connection and smiled to himself contentedly. He was convinced that Tel Aviv had understood the message.

Three weeks later, when the Pan-Arabian plane landed at Maza Airport, El-Hafez came out happy and smiling, though slightly weak and leaning on the arm of a stewardess.

TV cameras whirred, reporters showered a barrage of questions, but all El-Hafez had to say boiled down to a few words on his convalescence.

"It wasn't a talking trip, it was a health trip."

"Did his Excellency the President take advantage of his stay in Paris to hold talks with high-ranking persons?"

"The Foreign Office wanted to organize a number of meetings," El-Hafez explained, "but the doctor prescribed a complete rest. I didn't receive anyone."

"Has the ground at least been cleared for direct talks at the next meeting?"

"Quite possibly," El-Hafez sighed. "But it's too early to talk about it."

"Is France our ally?" one reporter queried.

"It would be impudent of me to say no. Almost certainly the day that France becomes persuaded of our strength and our ability to conduct the policy of the region, it will support us much more than it now supports Israel."

The press conference was over.

Cohn hurried over to El-Hafez and affectionately laid a hand on his shoulder.

"How do you feel now—after the operation and the onslaught of the reporters?"

"I'd like to be at home. There I'll feel fine," El-Hafez whispered in his friend's ear.

The presidential company, with Elie sitting beside El-Hafez in the car, traversed the streets of Damascus, at the very hour when Radio Damascus was broadcasting the news of the President's arrival.

A long hour later, the Voice of Israel news in Arabic carried a comprehensive report of El-Hafez' trip.

Elie knew how to make use of every piece of information and to transmit it to Israel without its passing through censorship, as was customary in the case of foreign correspondents and local journalists.

When the news leak become known to El-Hafez, he went into a rage. He ordered his Secret Service to open an investigation to find out the source of the leaks in the top echelons of the regime.

"There's no doubt that one of their men is here among us," Colonel El-Tayara raged. "I'd like to know how much the Zionists are paying him for his dirty work."

"Since we're dealing with persons close to the regime," El-Hafez said, "it would be better if the investigation is handled with kid gloves. No one must know that the Secret Service is starting to get suspicious. It will remain a secret between the two of us."

"Naturally, sir," El-Tayara said. "I'll do everything in order to disclose the traitor—and delicately."

El-Hafez brooded deeply.

He tried to conjure up the image of the traitor in his imagination. But it didn't help. There was no doubt that, thanks to the man's information, Israel knew everything that was going on in Damascus, on the Syrian Heights, and the Banias.

The more he thought about it, the more anxious he grew. It started gnawing into him. He swore with his heart to take revenge on the man who had managed to lead him and his government astray.

Who was he?

He decided to try an experiment.

The next day he urgently summoned the heads of the regime, held a secret meeting, and forbade those present to divulge what had been said to journalists or anyone else.

That same noon he turned the dial of his radio to the Voice of Israel's Arabic station, and was astonished to hear detailed information on that morning's meeting.

"What in the name of Allah!" El-Hafez muttered and summoned El-Tayara.

"Did you know about our secret meeting this morning?" he asked.

"No," El-Tayara replied. "But I heard about it a few minutes ago on the Arabic broadcast of the Israeli radio."

"Think for a moment. There were thirty officers at that meeting. If the details of the meeting were leaked to Israel so quickly, it could have been done either by a secret telegram or else by radio. Radio seems the greater likelihood. No one would risk sending a telegram through the scissors of Colonel Bakri."

Elie's first suspicions that something wasn't right in the regime were aroused around October, 1964. El-Hafez wasn't the devoted friend he used to be and showed a tendency to seclusion. To his friends he explained that the Baath was in a tight spot, and that enemy elements were sabotaging the regime.

In his opinion, they were forces operating under the inspiration of that intriguer Nasser.

The atmosphere grew more and more troubled. The heads of the regime were reserved, and nothing was like it used to be.

Elie reported to Tel Aviv: "Things are starting to get hot. I'm coming over."

And then, in the middle of October, he left for Paris and from there to Israel.

The information that had been transmitted to Israel was wonderfully accurate. The Israeli army knew how to translate it into action in the border incident of Wednesday, November 13, 1964.

That day, Syrian positions opened fire on Israeli tractors working land in Israeli territory. The Israeli response was not long in coming. A tank and heavy artillery force returned fire and silenced several emplacements in the sector.

But the Syrians didn't give up so easily. Fire was leveled from all sides, and there was no alternative but to call in the Air Force. Jet fighters and heavy bombers wiped out the Syrian positions and destroyed the diversion channels of the Jordan together with their earth-moving equipment.

Syrian propaganda, which had waxed arrogant about the effectiveness of the new MIG fighters and Syria's ability to wipe out any enemy on land or in the air, suffered a crushing defeat. The Israeli hits were right on the button. The effectiveness of the blow was maximal. World press support for Israel's reaction forced the Syrians to tighten their security belt and to reveal the secret of the terrible defeat.

It was clear that someone on the inside was leaking out information.

Too much information.

At that time, Elie Cohn was on home leave in Israel.

The thread of suspicion reached all the way to his home.

"When do you think you're going to stop all this running around in Europe?" Maurice, Elie's brother, asked him the evening he arrived in Israel.

Elie shrugged.

"Believe me, I'd like to get it over with and stay at home with you."

He looked at his brother a moment.

"Tell me, Maurice, is Mother at home?"

"Yes, she's on the roof, hanging out laundry. Shall we go up and surprise her?"

"No," Elie said. "We'll wait till she comes down."

Sophie, Elie's elderly mother, came in and her eyes shone with joy on seeing her beloved son.

"*Ya-Aini* (Upon my eyes)!" she cried in Arabic. "How we've missed you!"

"I'm here. There's nothing to worry about," Elie replied in Arabic with a Syrian accent.

Maurice looked at him.

"Where did you pick up that accent, Elie?" he asked.

"What's wrong?" Elie replied. "Most of the Arabs in Europe speak that way."

"You have connections with Arab merchants?"

Elie nodded.

"Frequently," he said, casually.

Sophie interrupted the dialogue. "Have you eaten, Elie?"

He went to his mother, leaned over, and kissed her on the forehead.

"The truth is I don't feel like eating, but if you make me something ·special the way only you know how, I'd enjoy eating."

"Do you want what we used to eat in Haleb? Something you like?"

"No, Mother," Elie said indifferently. "Find something else. I eat that dish pretty often."

Maurice looked puzzled.

"How do you get to eat it in Europe?"

"Why not?" Elie answered without hesitation. "Haven't you heard that in Europe they have all kinds of restaurants?"

Maurice blinked.

"Could be. I've never been to Europe."

"It's too bad," Elie consoled him. "Maybe I'll arrange for you to take a trip with me sometime. Europe is a wonderful continent for trips. I especially enjoyed my visits to Italy, Spain, and Germany. Incidentally, speaking of Germany, I forgot that I brought Sophie a great big doll that talks and smiles and squeaks."

He hurried to the suitcases, took out a doll, and showed it to Maurice.

Maurice looked at it in amazement.

"The Germans are experts at fine work," Elie remarked.

"But this isn't German," Maurice interrupted. "It says here 'Made in France.' "

Elie grinned lightly, took the doll from his brother's hands, and looked at the label.

"The crooks!" he declared. "They sell a French doll in Germany as if it had a German patent."

Maurice laughed derisively.

"I don't think you know where you bought that doll. Since you left Israel, you've gotten more and more mixed up."

"Could be," Elie said in a low voice. "After all, they didn't send me to Europe to buy dolls and toys."

"Don't be sore, Elie," Maurice said with genuine respect for his brother. "But I don't believe that *all* you're doing in Europe is acquisitions."

"What are you getting at?" Elie asked. "Do you suspect me of something?"

Little Sophie came into the room and fell into her father's arms.

"Daddy!" she cried. "Where have you been all this time?"

"At work," Elie replied, kissing her cheek.

"Work?" she asked. "So why do all the kids' daddies who go to work come home every day?"

"I work far away, Sophie. I can't come home every day. Look, I've brought you a big doll. Just like Sophie."

"Doll like Sophie?" the little girl asked.

Elie nodded.

"Yes, a doll like Sophie."

The little girl looked at the big doll that opened and shut its eyes. Then she cautiously touched the doll's hands, stuck a finger in its eyes, and in the end fell in love with her new toy and was oblivious to what went on around her.

Elie pulled over a chair from the table and sat down. His

mother came into the room with steaming cups of coffee, which she set before her two sons.

"Coffee from the good days," she said.

They sipped the fragrant beverage.

"It's great," Elie remarked.

"Everything Mother makes is great. Just being back home is something else. Right, Elie?" Maurice said.

"Yes," Elie sighed, his gaze fixed on the ceiling. "To be here is something else."

The door chime interrupted his train of reflections. Maurice went to open the door, took little Iris from Nadia's arms, and winked at her knowingly.

"Don't tell me. I can feel it in your face," Nadia cried and burst into the room like a storm.

"Elie!" she cried, as they fell into each other's arms in a moving embrace.

"Elie. I love you! Elie . . ."

She suddenly pulled back, examined his face, and returned to his arms.

"Tell me, when did you get in, and how?"

His lips caressed her cheek and kissed her earlobe.

"I arrived a few minutes ago, on a direct flight from Italy. I've got an unlimited leave."

"Unlimited leave?"

"Yes, till further notice."

Now it was his turn to give her a long, curious look. "How does *he* feel?" he asked, indicating her stomach.

"He? What makes you think it's a *he*?"

"It's time, isn't it, Nadia?"

She smiled.

"Yes. You know, girls first are a sign for boys."

"You owe me a son. I'm starting to feel isolated here among all you girls."

Nadia smiled tenderly.

"Come and see what I brought you."

He poured out the contents of his suitcase on the sofa and showed them the abundance of presents.

"I've brought you Chinese glass statuettes."

"China?" Maurice said. "What's with you and China?"

"Well, I forgot to tell you. A little over two months ago I was in China. In Europe there's nothing easier than to hop over to China. All the major airlines have flights to the Far

East, and from Hong Kong to China isn't far, especially if you have connections like mine."

To strengthen the impression, Elie pulled out a packet of photos. In one of them he was seen standing beside Chou En-lai.

"From these pictures," Maurice remarked, "one might imagine that China is a small town where the Prime Minister lets himself be photographed with every visitor."

"It depends, of course, on who the visitor is and the purpose of his visit. The Chinese, as you probably know, have always been a very hospitable people."

"I'm starting to doubt your job is real," Maurice said. "It seems like a very complicated business."

He cast a questioning look at Nadia.

"What do you think of your Marco Polo?" he asked.

"I don't know," she said. "I haven't had time to think."

From that moment, when suspicions started to penetrate his house, Elie became introverted and nervous. He wasn't the same animated man everyone remembered.

One evening, shortly before the birth of his son, Shaul, while Nadia was in her birth pangs, Elie sat down beside her and with eyes enveloped in sadness poured out his heart to her.

"I know this time it'll be a boy. It's not for nothing you're having a difficult birth," he said, and patted her head. "But a son will be suitable compensation."

His voice choked for a moment. "You'll be happy, Nadia."

She looked at him in wonder. "Why do you say, *You'll be happy, Nadia?* Aren't you happy at the birth of your son?"

"Well, what I meant was that you have a right to see the son we've been waiting for so long."

She caught Elie by the hand and said insistently, "Tell me the truth, Elie. What's troubling you? What are you so worried about?"

He sighed. "I'm sick of this wandering around. I want to get the job over with and come back home for good."

"So why don't you do it?" she asked.

"I have a contract till May, 1965. Till the eve of our eighteenth Independence Day."

Her eyes were covered by a film of sadness and her nails dug into his palm.

"Take me to the hospital, Elie. I feel that very soon I'll bring you the son you've been waiting for."

He went to the phone, called a taxi, and took her to the hospital.

The next morning he learned he had a son.

"Now," he said when the family came to visit, "we have a man in the house to balance things out a bit."

Nadia smiled happily. Elie was proud of his son. She knew that he had been waiting for this moment impatiently. She also knew that it wouldn't be long before Elie would leave her again.

They held a gay traditional circumcision ceremony, and two weeks later Elie again packed his bags and kissed his wife and children good-bye.

The anxious looks in their innocent eyes as they met Elie's seemed to portend that this was the last time they would meet.

10

Caught!

Elie flew to Zurich, and then to Argentina, where he spent four days in Buenos Aires. Then he returned to Damascus.

The reception in the Syrian capital was somewhat cool.

His familiars, and among them Salem Saif and Sheikh El-Ard, told him of the terrible rout suffered on the border.

Elie, as a patriot, burst out in anger. "What's the party waiting for? It's time to open a second front and put an end to the Israeli aggression. Israel is the most despicable enemy of Arab nationalism. It ought to be eliminated once and for all."

"Yes," Salem Saif muttered. "But our army isn't ready yet. And the other Arab countries are quarreling with one another. Arab nationalism is suffering from hardening of the arteries and internal noncooperation."

They accompanied him home. There, over a cup of coffee, Salem unrolled before him the events of the previous weeks.

"The entire deviation project, in which we've invested millions, is to be postponed because of the Israeli terrorist action of the thirteenth of this month."

"Why did they open fire?" Elie asked.

"I very much fear," Saif said, "that it was a few hot-headed officers on our side who opened fire."

"Why?"

Saif drank the rest of his coffee, and spoke in an even lower voice.

"Lately there's been a great deal of tension in the top leadership. Things aren't what they used to be. People are aloof and uncommunicative. Especially since you left. You're the one with the approach and the connections with everyone. All that dissipation and freedom of action resulted in a situation where they belittled the strength of Israel. They had to increase the tension and the alertness by some border shooting. But nobody expected such a strong reaction from the other side, much less such direct hits on our vital points."

87

"You think there's an underground espionage movement here?" Elie asked.

"I don't know. Could be. Even though I haven't heard about it from an official source."

"What does it say in that propaganda you have to broadcast?"

"Same thing as usual. They want to organize capital and public opinion for the Arab cause."

"Nothing else?"

"Nothing else."

Elie sensed his position was worsening. He knew he could be arrested any day. But once in the espionage business, he couldn't get out again. The show had to go on.

He had promised Nadia that he would finish his assignment by May, 1965. But he knew, just as Headquarters in Tel Aviv knew, and as Nadia sensed, that it would never end.

His ensuing broadcasts to Israel were shorter, and it wasn't hard to understand why. Nevertheless, his connections with the top brass didn't weaken. The internal tension in Damascus didn't affect him. And information continued to flow into his hands.

One evening there was a knock on his door. It was his good friend Salim Khatoum.

"I've got a break from Headquarters," he said. "And I've got an urge for some action. Do you think you could fix something up for me?"

Elie looked at him in amazement.

"You're turning me into a pimp, Salim," he said smiling. "I do it only when I organize parties at my home, but I'm not a purveyor of call girls, Colonel."

Khatoum blinked.

"Excuse me, Kamel," he apologized in embarrassment. "I didn't mean it. It's just that I've been under a terrible strain the past month. I've hardly been outside Headquarters. They're making some changes in structure. You know, equipment and command plans."

"Why are you telling me this, Salim?" Elie asked suspiciously.

"It's no secret," Salim said. "You can look out your window and see everything happening down there," he continued.

Elie grinned.

"Too bad I didn't think of it," he said. "From this house you can make a revolution."

"Forget about it, Kamel. Come, let's have something to

eat. Life is too short to keep worrying about tomorrow."

Elie indicated the liquor counter.

"The bar's at your disposal. Help yourself."

He went up to the bar and looked over the bottles until he found his favorite.

"What'll you have?" he asked. "I see there's half a bottle of real vodka here. I tried this a little while ago at the Russian attache's. It left a powerful impression."

"The attache or the vodka?"

"Mainly the vodka," Khatoum replied. "Shall we drink to the health of the Baath?"

He pulled out the cork and filled the glasses to the brim. They clinked and he tossed the drink down his gullet.

"If you're drinking vodka," he said, "then all at one gulp. That's what the attache taught me, and I'd say he's right."

"I prefer to enjoy a drink my own way," Elie said. "I'll take it slowly, if you don't mind."

Salim snooped around in the kitchen pantry, where he found a smoked Argentine salami. He began peeling it.

"Life certainly is strange," he said, as if to himself. "A hundred meters from Headquarters, and we're in a different world."

Elie looked at him, puzzled, and Khatoum explained.

"There at Headquarters it's like a volcano about to explode, but here, at your place, everything's so peaceful and intimate."

"What's going on, Salim?"

"First, the new decisions that were taken at the party meeting. Secondly, new security arrangements, with new equipment coming into the Ministry of Defense and the Army."

He bit off a piece of the smoked salami.

"I once told you, as an army man I don't meddle in politics. But at the last meeting I realized the close connection between army and politics. Anyway, in order to annoy this pestilence called Israel, it's been decided to disturb its sleep by sending in saboteurs."

Elie nodded.

"These saboteurs," Khatoum went on, "will be recruited from among the youths of Syria and Gaza. They will be trained in modern warfare. Their trainers will be the same Algerian guerrillas who made life miserable for the French up to the eve of the evacuation.

"If you ask me," Khatoum added suddenly, "it's the most

refined and harmless solution for the Baath's policy. A little terror will drive the Jews crazy, but won't alert the world to stand beside them or denounce us."

Elie reflected a moment before digesting the new information, then he smiled disparagingly.

"So that's what all the noise and tension around here's been about?"

"That's not all, but more than that I'm afraid I can't tell you, Kamel."

Elie spent the remaining few hours before dawn in gloomy thought. Despite the fact that he broadcast very frequently, sometimes twice a day, he knew how to distinguish the important items. What Colonel Salim Khatoum had just told him had not yet been sufficiently digested in his mind. He waited for morning before broadcasting the item to his superiors.

Just before eight A.M. Elie removed the cover from the transistor and uncovered the sending key. In a slow rhythm, on a fixed frequency, he broadcast to Headquarters in Tel Aviv.

In the broadcast, Elie said he had heard from Khatoum about a plan to set up a brigade of Palestinian commandos headed by Syrian officers, who would carry out sabotage missions in Israel. The plan was to be Pan-Arabic and grass roots in nature, like the war in Algeria.

Elie waited a moment for the answer from Tel Aviv confirming the broadcast. However, instead of the confused whistle which would signify receipt of the transmission, he heard fists pounding on his door.

He leaped from his seat, instinctively sheltering the small transmitter in his arms. Facing him were a group of security agents in plain clothes. Their guns were leveled directly at him:

"Don't move!" one of them yelled.

An officer in an army uniform came forward from among the party of invaders. Elie didn't have any trouble recognizing him—Colonel Ahmed Swidani, head of Syrian Intelligence and Counterespionage.

He went up, snatched the radio out of Elie's hand, and smiled glumly.

"So we've finally caught up with you."

Only then did Elie realize the full significance of the scene, though his alert mind refused to accept the new reality. He tried to save whatever could still be saved.

"Gentlemen," he said, "you're mistaken. I'm an Arab immigrant from Argentina."

"We've already heard that story," the Colonel yelled, his excitement evident in his voice. "Now tell us what your real name is."

"Kamel Amin Tabet, an Arab immigrant from Argentina."

"So be it," Swidani said in a low voice. "Kamel Amin Tabet, you are under arrest."

He motioned to two of the men in the room, and then hissed between his teeth, "I promise you that within a few hours we'll know who you are and what you're doing here in Syria. Now move!"

Two of Swidani's men put handcuffs on his wrists. The guns leveled at him by the rest convinced him that there was no sense resisting. Even if he still maintained a feeble hope, his sixth sense told him that all was lost.

Before they left the room, Swidani went over to the little table on which he broadcast to Tel Aviv, and found a wireless message that had been received that morning.

Tel Aviv (it read) *wants additional information on . . .*

There it stopped.

"Strange," the Colonel muttered, looking at the small transistorized transmitter. "Who would have thought that a tiny set like this could reach Tel Aviv."

Then, as he thought of Tel Aviv, he smiled in satisfaction.

"There's no doubt about it. Kamel Amin Tabet, whatever his real name is, is a Zionist spy." His rage mounted as he recalled Tabet's close connections with the top leadership. His eyes were like hot rivets in his face; when he opened and closed his mouth, it looked like a steel trap.

"Filthy dog!" he cried in a strangled voice. "You'll die. Tell the whole truth! Who's helping you? Where are the other Zionist spies in Damascus?"

Cohn remained impassive.

"No one's helping me," he said calmly. "I don't know any Zionist spies in Damascus. Everything I did, I did on my own —with the help of this transmitter."

One of Swidani's assistants came into the room and interrupted the conversation by showing the colonel a package of Yardley soap.

"Look what I found inside the soap," the man said. "Explosives and three packages of poison."

Swidani looked straight into Cohn's eyes.

"It's a good thing we caught you now. What the hell," he cursed, "you thought you'd do a bit of sabotaging too?"

"You're wrong," Elie interrupted him. "I had no intention of doing any sabotage in Damascus. This material was in case I got caught. If things hadn't worked out the way they did, I would have blcwn up the transmitter and all the equipment in the room. That's the whole truth."

In a careful search of the house, an additional transmitter was discovered. This find, however, was not important.

Colonel Ahmed Swidani sat down on the sofa and thought for a moment. Then he called his assistant, Second Lieutenant Adnan Tabra and whispered a few words in his ear.

A few minutes later one of the soldiers came over to Elie and removed his handcuffs. Everyone but the colonel, his assistant, and one bodyguard then left the room silently.

"Listen carefully, Kamel," the colonel said after a few minutes. "If we drag you out of here in broad daylight, the whole country will know it in a few minutes. It's better if we do it after dark. Meanwhile we'll hold the interrogation right here."

And so, in the bedroom, beside the table on which he had so many times broadcast to Tel Aviv, the interrogation of Elie Cohn began. The colonel and his men were convinced that Kamel was merely an Arab working for the Israeli Security Service, rather than a Jew born and bred.

That evening, when the time came for the broadcast, Swidani got up and leveled his gun at Cohn.

"I want you to braodcast the following item to Tel Aviv," he barked. "And don't try to get smart. We have a code expert who can easily spot anything fishy."

"Colonel," Cohn cried, "you are forcing me to do something against my will, which as a prisoner I am not compelled to do."

The colonel came over and slapped his face.

"Do what I tell you! And don't tell me about the rights of a spy."

Elie Cohn went up to the transmitter and Colonel Ahmed Swidani instructed him what to say. "The Syrian army is in a state of alert."

Elie started transmitting, covered by three loaded pistols and under the watchful eye of the Syrian code expert.

Elie transmitted the item, but at a different speed than usual. Thus Tel Aviv learned—as previously agreed upon—that Elie Cohn had been captured.

"Did he do it right?" the suspicious colonel asked the code expert.

The man nodded.

11

The Interrogations

At that moment, two hundred kilometers away, the broadcast was picked up, and the technicians beside the receiving set were shocked.

"Elie Cohn's been caught!" one of the radiomen cried.

The man in charge of the night shift called the head of the network, and as he heard the voice on the other side, reported laconically: "Our man in Damascus has been arrested."

From that moment instructions began to flow in rapidly. The technicians received orders to pretend they hadn't understood the transmission and at the same time to try to clarify what had happened. Everyone waited tensely for the next broadcast. It wasn't long in coming.

The next morning at eight the radio again buzzed in the communications room of Tel Aviv Headquarters. Elie Cohn was again on the line, this time at his usual rate of transmission. But Tel Aviv hinted in its reply that it understood what had happened.

When he heard the sentence "We did not receive your transmissions yesterday and this morning, try again this evening," Cohn knew that Tel Aviv knew.

Colonel Swidani derived satisfaction from his sly game. He decided to stay in Elie's villa another evening in order to play with Tel Aviv.

"They've fallen into the trap," he said with satisfaction. "We mustn't let on that we've caught their man."

When it came time for the next broadcast—after a day of exhaustive interrogation—doubt began to creep into Elie's mind. Maybe Tel Aviv really hadn't understood, as the Colonel had tried to persuade him. In the next broadcast he again tapped his message at a faster pace than usual, meaning "I've been caught. Don't believe the broadcasts."

Tel Aviv knew now for sure, and wanted to gain time. They joined the Tel Aviv-Damascus game until the broadcast of Sunday, January 24, 1965.

That day, after Colonel Swidani had received authorization from President El-Hafez to publicize the capture of the Zionist spy, he ordered Elie to broadcast the following announcement to Tel Aviv:

To the director of the security service in Tel Aviv
Kamel Amin Tabet and his friends are our guests in Damascus. We are waiting for you to send us their colleagues.

Signed:
Syrian Espionage Service
end

A short time later, Radio Damascus began a devil's dance, as the announcer proclaimed at the beginning of the nine o'clock news that the Syrian Security Services had caught Kamel Amin Tabet, one of the most important Israeli agents operating in Damascus.

The news spread throughout Damascus like a brush fire. No words could describe the shock that came over the top Syrian leadership. The thousands of people who had met Kamel Amin Tabet at parties or on business began to question themselves. Fear took hold of them.

No one wanted to believe that Kamel—the darling of the administration and candidate for a minister's post in the Baath government, the millionaire envied by all, and noted philanthropist—was a spy.

And for the hated Zionist state at that.

The order that reached Investigation Headquarters of the Syrian Secret Police shortly afterward was short and to the point.

"Do everything to get Kamel to talk. Don't flinch from any means."

The message was signed by General Amin El-Hafez, President of the Republic and Elie's personal friend.

When the telephones started disturbing the peace of the top leaders with all sorts of questions, El-Hafez decided to question his traitor friend Kamel himself, in the torture chambers of Sheba'im Prison, in the army camp near Damascus.

He entered the accused's cell under heavy guard. When he came out an hour later, he was shocked and shaken.

"What's wrong, General?" Ahmed Swidani asked worriedly.

"It's incredible," El-Hafez mumbled. "It's incredible. Kamel isn't even a Moslem. I asked him a few religious questions. I was amazed to learn that Kamel isn't a Moslem at all. He knew very little about the Koran and when I asked him to quote me the *Fat'ha,** he mumbled a couple of broken sentences. He apologized, saying that he had forgotten a few lines because many years had passed since he had prayed seriously. Only then did I realize that Kamel Amin Tabet is a Jew."

"A Jew!" the colonel cried.

"Maybe even an Israeli from Israel," El-Hafez mumbled fearfully.

The colonel stiffened.

"Give me five hours, General, and, by Allah, I'll tell you who the man is."

The evening paper came out with splash headlines, but revealed little about the arrest. It dwelt on the simple news item that had been broadcast over Radio Damascus news. The sensational headline read:

Important Israeli spy arrested. The most dangerous agent in past 20 years

In his Damascus home, Amin El-Hafez paced the floor, confused and depressed. He waited fearfully and with growing nervousness for the reaction from Cairo. It was clear to him that Cairo would find in Elie Cohn an instrument to attack the ruling junta, and, first and foremost, himself.

After a while he phoned the commander of the army, the Syrian Chief of Staff, and instructed him to put his units on a state of alert, for any eventuality.

Even in the middle of his capital and his army he didn't trust a soul. He expected a possible army uprising from unknown quarters.

The reaction of the Arab world opposed to the Baath regime was not long in coming. Unexpectedly, it was Iraq that reacted first with an excited broadcast, telling of the capture of the Israeli agent.

"Hafez is a coward!" the Radio Baghdad announcer cried. "He won't allow a public trial. He's afraid of a scandal that will bring down his regime."

* The opening chapter of the Koran.

Radio Cairo was quick to follow.

"Damascus," Radio Cairo exclaimed, "is completely confused because of the merchant from Argentina who managed to deceive the entire Baath leadership and their supporters. The day is not far off when Hafez will enter Maza Jail and join his good friend Elie Cohn."

In order to point up the scandal in the best oriental tradition, a song was composed with verses and a chorus sung by a men's choral group. Every time someone in the song asked, "Where's the Baath?" the chorus responded, "In Maza."

El-Hafez lost control of himself. Just as in the McCarthy witch-hunt era, all the security services and secret bodies were activated on a giant manhunt, and a relentless campaign of revenge.

Interrogations in the basement of the Damascus jail broke all records for cruelty, and criminals, who at any other time would have got only a few years, now were given long sentences—or death. The military and civil courts of Damascus in a short period sent more people to the next world than during long years previously, and this in a country where executions were very popular events.

The El-Hafez witch-hunt made no distinction between traitors, spies, and ordinary criminals. All were charged with sabotaging the regime, and as such went to the scaffold.

The Syrian interrogation officer apparently had been trained by the Gestapo. He had a dull expression and well-manicured fingernails.

"The time has come for you to open your mouth, Cohn," the man said, his soft-spoken words pounding like hammers.

"I have nothing more to say," Elie said quietly. "Besides, even if I wanted to, I could add nothing to what I've already said."

The officer came up to him with a threatening expression.

"They want you alive for the trial, and they want you normal enough to know what you're saying. So don't make me hurt you so much that you'll lose your mind."

Elie smiled wryly.

"It's good you told me that. Now I know that you can't do anything to me before the trial."

The officer glared at him.

"Listen, Cohn. You're an ugly ape, especially when you smile." Then he slapped Elie's face sharply.

Cohn turned his head and bit his lip.

"It won't help. I'm not talking."

He recalled what he had been taught, and planned the only possible course of action. He started taking slow, deep breaths, to suffuse his blood with oxygen, and gradually flexed the muscles of his arms, thighs, and stomach. Tensed, relaxed, tensed, relaxed, to increase the oxygen absorption and to step up the circulation.

The officer looked at his assistant.

"What do you say, Muhzi?"

"You don't know those Jews!" the man said. "They'd rather die than talk. Especially since you can't put on too much pressure. Besides, he's half unconscious. He won't say anything more today. Pain won't affect him. I suggest we continue tomorrow."

"No!" the officer cried. "We can't put it off just like that. Give me a moment to think. I'll make him talk!"

Late that night, the door of the cell opened and someone came in. Elie awoke to the blinding light of a large flashlight.

"Get up, Cohn," a voice barked from behind the beam of light. "You have a few things to remember before you open your mouth tomorrow."

The voice of the speaker came to him from a distance. It sounded vague and monotonous. Elie was too dazed to identify it. The speaker instructed Elie not to open his mouth and to avoid mentioning his close connections with the army.

"Remember," he heard dimly, "the army is at odds within itself. If they try to get you to confess your connections with certain officers, don't tell them anything. You don't know anyone and you're not connected with them."

Elie shaded his eyes with his hand and mumbled in a faint voice, "Who are you?"

"It doesn't matter. Think of me as one of the persons you've met. I may be Salim, Zaher, Mahmoud. I'm everyone who's ever been connected with you. I can even be El-Hafez. Think of me and all of them and keep your mouth shut."

The light went out. When he managed to focus his eyes, there was nobody there. Only the echoes of the footsteps of a group of people moving away sounded from the top of the stairs.

The next day, after an exhausting period of questioning, the interrogation officer managed to find out that the previous night certain people had tried to convince Elie not to talk.

"Did you see who they were?" the officer asked.

"No. I couldn't see a thing."

"But you could have recognized the voice. There's no doubt that the man is known to you."

"They surprised me. And they spoke in muffled and threatening tones. I don't think I could have recognized them even if I had been completely awake."

The officer turned to Muhzi.

"How does he sound to you?" he asked. "To me it looks as if he's daydreaming."

Muhzi shook his head.

"Not Elie Cohn."

He went over to Elie, sat down beside him, and offered him a cigarette.

"Come, tell us all about it from the beginning. It sounds very interesting."

The dress rehearsal for the big spectacle of the hanging of Elie Cohn was the Attasi affair, which began as another Damascus whodunit televised to the sound of John Phillip Sousa marches, and came to its gruesome conclusion on March 5, 1965, a short time after the opening of the trial of Elie Cohn.

In the cool early morning hours, Farhan Attasi, a Syrian with American citizenship, was led out to Al-Marjah Square and hanged. A giant poster was attached to his white condemned-man's robe, citing the verdict.

For seven whole hours the body swung from the scaffold, while thousands of curious citizens stood and watched. Then it was cut down and buried.

Attasi's uncle and partner in espionage on behalf of the Americans, Lieutenant-Colonel Abdul Muin Hakemi, forty-three, was executed by a firing squad in the courtyard of a Damascus army barracks.

The Syrians accused Attasi of receiving from Hakemi eleven shells of a new Soviet antiaircraft gun that had been recently introduced into the Syrian army. He had handed them over to Walter Snowdon, second secretary of the Amercan Embassy in Damascus, who had been expelled from Syria.

Washington denied the charges, but not very vigorously, preferring to put the emphasis on the harsh treatment to which Attasi had been subjected.

Among other things, Attasi had been "treated" by means of electrodes, blows, brainwashing, and starving. American

officials had not been permitted to visit him in prison and he
had been allowed no lawyer. Only carefully censored portions
of his secret trial had been televised.

Despite all the special treatment, it was impossible to play
back any part of the trial, or to show scenes from it without
discerning the terror on the face of the accused.

More than once the blood-curdling scream was heard: "No!
Don't take me to the electric room!"

All this, however, didn't help. The faltering Baath regime
was determined to outdo Nasser in a hate campaign against
America.

Daily the radio, newspapers, and television denounced the
United States for what the Minister of Information Mashhour
Zeitoun called "The American policy of sabotage and espio-
nage in Syria."

That evening, when it was clear beyond a doubt that Elie
Cohn, Agent 088 in Damascus, had been arrested by the Syrian security services, the phone rang in the home of the Cohn
family in Bat-Yam, and the voice that kept up contact between the family and Elie while he was out of the country,
said sadly, "Nadia, Shim'on here. Elie Cohn has been
arrested."

The man didn't add anything more, but the heavy campaign to save his life was already in full swing.

Israel Intelligence initiated the trip to Paris of Nadia and
her two children, and organized a giant press conference at
which Nadia declared that her husband had fallen victim of a
despicable plot, and that she was prepared to do anything to
save him, if not for herself then at least for her children, and
the baby who had not known his father.

The picture of Nadia holding her two children in her arms
won the sympathy of France and all Europe.

For the first time in the history of espionage, the veil of secrecy was lifted and the country that employed Elie came out
in an open struggle to save him with all means at its command.

They hired a noted lawyer, Jacques Mercier, one of the
leading French attorneys, to defend Elie. The background
was explained to him, he was given particulars on the structure of the ruling junta and the possibilities of acquittal.

For the first time in his career, Mercier was assigned to
conduct negotiations with two enemy states having no common language between them.

A former paratrooper in the French army and an avowed

Gaullist, Mercier agreed to take on what appeared to him at first sight as impossible.

Damascus wasn't expecting him. All the bureaus concerned delicately avoided the question of an attorney for Elie Cohn.

Amin El-Hafez, the man who could have had the final say, was on convalescent leave. Apart from him, no one thorized to give the okay. It was a sinister beginning.

Damascus was seized with fear and terror. Mercier sighed as he recalled the tune "Damascus Rock" composed by Duke Ellington, during his goodwill tour of the Arab states, in the middle of the revolution of 1963.

12

The Trial—First Phase

"The Arab people, citizens of Syria," the chief justice began. "What you will hear in this trial are incisive facts and exact particulars, as provided in the investigation of the Israeli spy Elie Cohn, the Zionist's greatest spy, who was sent into Syria to subvert the regime. We have no doubts as to the facts of the crime, and you my brothers will be able to consider the gravity of this man's crime in the course of the trial."

From his lofty position in the prisoner's dock, Elie could hear the speaker faintly. He didn't allow the crowd's angry reactions to occupy his thoughts for long. He knew that he had to concentrate all his powers on the words of the investigating judge, and to try to answer him decisively and unequivocally—to the extent that he was able.

It was clear to him that his sentence was sealed, even before he had been brought to the prisoner's dock. But when he got there, straight from the torture chambers of the Damascus prison, he still had fight in him—and desire to shatter publicly the aura of sanctity that surrounded the officers' junta.

The rough voice of the judge, Colonel Sallah Dali, interrupted his thoughts.

"The accused, Eliyahu Ben Shaul Cohn of Tel Aviv, Israel. Is that your real name?"

"That's my name."

"Do you recognize anyone in the panel of judges sitting here?"

Elie looked up and to the right, then looked straight ahead of him, toward the judges' bench.

He saw out of the corner of his eye the row of judges and the grave expression of Colonel Salim Khatoum. A slight shiver ran down his spine, and his left cheek twitched slightly.

"No, sir," he said. "I don't recognize anyone."

"But Radio Baghdad claims that Salim Khatoum, sitting beside me, was your friend."

"That's the first time I've heard of it," Elie said laconically

"Do you mean to say that there are madmen sitting in Baghdad?"

"Madmen or agents."

The chief justice started to boil over.

"Agents like you, eh?" he roared.

"I don't know," Cohn muttered. "I'm only an envoy."

"Sure, you're an envoy!" Colonel Sallah Dali yelled angrily. "You were given a job to do and you're doing it. The others are merely out for money. You have a good friend by the name of Hashem Abu-Zaher, from the Lebanese paper *Al Mouhrar*. He's on your side."

Colonel Dali was silent for a moment, then cleared his throat and continued.

"I might also mention Kemal Marawa, owner of *Al Hiyyat*. These agents get payment from Israel to defend you and smear us. The money that your government throws around is *our* money. It came from our oil which is diverted into Israel by those agents."

Dali's words were interrupted by stormy applause from the court, accompanied by boos and hisses.

The chief justice lifted his hands and silence returned to the courtroom.

"I read in the Lebanese paper *Al Hiyyat* that all the officers in the Syrian army were your friends, Cohn," he went on. "Is that correct?"

"I knew only four officers."

"And Salim Khatoum among them?"

"I already told you that he wasn't," Elie said in a bored voice.

Salim Khatoum breathed easy.

Apart from the sharp eyes of the television camera, no one noticed it. Salim leaned over the table a moment, and wrote a note to his friend.

"Give this note to Amin," he ordered, and it was done.

The courtroom was still buzzing from Elie's answer. The judges did all they could to calm things down. When quiet returned a few moments later, Colonel Sallah Dali continued.

"Who were the four officers you were in contact with?"

Elie thought carefully for a moment and then said in a monotonous voice: "Mukadam Halil Safour, Suleiman al-Rajoula from the Security Service, Adal al-Sa'idi, a retired colonel, and Muhammad Daloul."

"And that's all?"

"No," Elie replied. "I was also in contact with lawyer

Mashir Houri and Ilia Al-Ma'az, a navigator at Damascus airport."

All eyes turned to Al-Ma'az, who sat with bowed head in the prisoner's dock. His colleague, Lawyer Mashir Houri, had died about a month before the opening of the trial, after a long illness.

"Which bureaus did you manage to penetrate?" the chief justice continued.

"The Ministry of Information, the broadcasting station, the Central Bank, the Ministry for Municipal Affairs, the Defense Ministry. I also visited El-Hama on the Israeli-Syrian border three times."

"And what about all your other friends?"

"I knew Baha ad-Din Rif'i from the Economy Ministry and Lieutenant Ma'azi, the uncle of General Ma'azi Zaher a-Din."

"What were your connections with Colonel Safour?"

"He once came to an official party I held in· my apartment," Elie related. "As a gesture of friendship, he invited me to a guided tour of the army base at Ladkiyeh. We toured the military installations in the port and I got a detailed explanation."

Colonel Dali swore at him between his teeth.

"Your Honor," Elie said suddenly. "Before I continue my testimony, I must insist on the rights of any accused man, namely, that I be given a lawyer."

Dali looked up in surprise.

"Impossible! You have more than enough defenders. All the corrupt press is your defense attorney. And that's plenty."

Elie grew deeply despondent again.

"Now, in the name of Allah," Dali shouted, "let's get on with the trial," he said, immediately adding, "Tell the court about yourself, and try to tell only the truth."

"Everything from the beginning?"

The judge nodded.

"You can add more information if you feel it's necessary," he remarked in derision.

"I was born in Alexandria in 1942," Elie began. "My parents, Shaul and Sophie Cohn, had immigrated there from Haleb before the First World War. We lived in a cheap apart ment in Duek Passage in the Jewish Quarter. My father made a bare living by working in the tie factory of the rich Jew Daniel Banin.

"In spite of the hardship at home, I did well at the public

school of the Jewish Community, and while my brothers left school one after the other, I continued studying at a French high school with the help of a grant I received. But my studies did not relieve me from the obligation to help support my family, and after school I worked as a salesman in the Clark clothing store.

"When the Rabbi of Alexandria, Dr. Moshe Ventura, set up an evening Yeshiva, I joined it without hesitation. I studied there diligently, and that's where I learned Hebrew.

"I attended the Faculty of Engineering at Farouk University for two years, but then—it was in 1951—riots broke out in Egypt against the British, and the Moslem Brothers put a stop to studies in the university with their demonstrations. I left my studies and went to work full time in the clothing store.

"After the War of Independence, in 1948, my father and mother and members of my family left Egypt and settled in Israel. As I was determined to finish my university studies, I didn't join them but remained in Egypt.

"My older sister, Odette, married first—to an official of the Pazgas Company. She lives in Bat-Yam. My brother Maurice works in the post office in Tel Aviv and lives in Ramat-Gan, and my third brother, Ezra, is also married and lives in Bat-Yam."

After a short pause Elie continued.

"In August, 1954, I was arrested as a suspected member of a Zionist spy ring. I was arrested with a great many other Jews and put in a detention camp near Cairo.

"It wasn't an easy life there, in the Egyptian ghetto. But it served me as sort of a springboard to get out of Egypt. All I had with me when I left was a suitcase with some old clothes.

"That's how I got to Naples. There we were received by a representative of the Jewish Agency, who put us up in a third-class hotel. Later, when all the documents were arranged, they brought us to Genoa by train, and from there we sailed to Israel.

"No one was waiting for me when I arrived except a man by the name of Peretz, who met me when I got off the boat and gave me the address of my relatives."

Elie filled his lungs with air, was silent for a moment, and then continued:

"Before I went to meet my family in Bat-Yam, I phoned my sister Odette. She, of course, was happy and moved to tears to hear my voice, and to learn that I was safe and sound, and in the Holy Land. All the time they had been worried that something had happened to me when I was expelled from Egypt.

"I looked for work and was directed to the Egyptian Immigrants Club in Tel Aviv. The club director, Sirmano, who studied with me at the Jewish school in Alexandria, gave me the address of an office in Allenby Street. It was a commercial office.

"The secretary there told me to wait until the manager arrived. When he appeared, I went into his office. He was an officer with the rank of captain, a man of medium height, brown hair, about thirty. He wanted to know if I was fluent in Arabic. Then he arranged for me to translate Arabic newspapers.

"That same officer sent me to an adjacent office, where another officer gave me an Arabic newspaper.

"I tried to translate it, but found that my knowledge of Hebrew wasn't sufficient. The officer said to me: 'You won't be able to translate, but you can index the newspapers.'"

"Did they give you classified material to translate?" Dali asked.

"Naturally," Elie replied. "The office did translations for the army."

"Were there daily papers too?" Dali asked with interest. "Papers that appeared that same day in Cairo or Damascus?"

Elie nodded.

"How do you get them?"

"The officer told me that every day the papers come in from all the Arab countries. Actually, the matter didn't interest me too much. I worked to support myself and did not want to get mixed up in things that didn't concern me."

"Tell me more about the office," Dali demanded.

"As I said, the office belonged to the army. The translators are Jews from Iraq and Egypt. In the room where I worked there were four translators; one of them was the man in charge. They called him Israel. I earned 170 pounds a month."

"How long did you work there?"

"I don't remember exactly," Elie said. "Anyway, not more than a few months. One day they told me that there wasn't enough work for me in the office."

"What did you do after you were dismissed?"

Elie shrugged his shoulders.

"I wandered around a few weeks without work. Then the

Ministry of Labor sent me to a bookkeeping course and a course in cost accounting. With the help of a friend from the Egyptian Immigrants, I got a job in the auditing department of the Hamashbir Hamerkazi on Salame Street in Tel Aviv. My job was to inspect the cooperative shops."

"And what happened then?"

"In that same period I met Nadia, through my sister-in-law. She was a young nurse of Iraqi origin. In 1959 we got married and bought an apartment on Rehov Hatehiya in Bat-Yam, on the Saving for Building Plan."

"And you managed to get by on a clerk's salary in the marketing company?"

"My wife also worked, and helped out as much as she could."

There was a long pause in the courtroom and then Dali said: "About that man who came to offer you a job in the Israeli Security Service. What can you tell us about him?"

"One day a man named Zalman came to see me. He told me that they had kept an eye on my work and found that I was suited to a more responsible task. He asked me if I was willing to work for Intelligence and to go to Europe or an Arab country."

"And you agreed?"

"I told him that I had just married, and didn't have the urge to travel. My wife was a nurse before we got married, but she had quit work when she became pregnant, and I had to work overtime."

"And then you agreed to be a spy?"

Elie lowered his eyes.

"I didn't know the nature of the new job I would be given. In any case, after I was fired from my job, I was ready for anything."

"But you probably understood that it involved a mission to an Arab country."

"Even if I understood, I didn't let it worry me. I could have left at any time. Zalman himself told me, 'Come and try intelligence work for six months. If you like it, stay, if not— you're free to do as you wish.' "

"And then they taught you everything about spying?"

"They did everything to prepare me to serve the State faithfully."

"And then they turned you into a Syrian citizen. An Arab merchant from Argentina."

"It wasn't especially difficult. I had trained for it a long time."

"And the matter of religion. What about that?"

Elie looked at the judge's face.

"For the purpose of learning the Moslem religion, I was introduced to a Moslem Kadi. He taught me the essentials of the religion of Mohammed, as far as I know them."

"And what if you had failed in the test of reality?"

"I would say that I wasn't an orthodox Moslem, and that I had vague religious memories from my school days."

Dali gave a growl of dissatisfaction. He thought to himself that if it hadn't been for a matter of chance, the Zionist spy would have continued on in his criminal activity. He looked straight at the accused and blasted out.

"Tell us what they taught you in the Koran."

"Five prayers a day, a section from the Koran, and the *Fat'ha* of the prayers."

"Why did they teach you the Moslem religion?"

"Because in my identity card it said that I was a Moslem."

"So you could be a devoted Jew, and a spy besides—is that right?"

The listeners smiled at Dali's last remark, and he immediately noted this, like an actor who feels the pulse of his audience.

"They told me the Moslem religion suited me better because the Christian religion was too complicated."

"In other words, you exploited religion in order to get into the spying business. You used religion to masquerade as a Moslem and to simplify your entrance into Syria."

Dali's fists clenched in anger.

"A pox on your house! God blinded you. Your masters in Israel forgot that they were slaughtered in the past when they used the Moslem religion. You forgot your history. Do you know the Talmud?"

"No, I'm not acquainted with it."

"You want to tell me they didn't teach you the Talmud?"

Cohn shook his head.

"And the Torah, do you know it, Cohn?"

"Yes."

"We all know the Torah, damn it, but why didn't they teach you the Talmud? Are those new Zionist instructions?"

"I don't know."

"Enough!" Dali cried. "You don't learn history, you don't

learn anything. Now tell me, who gave you the name Kamel Amin Tabet?"

"I don't remember, but they told me that my father's name was Amin and my mother was Sa'ida Ibrahim, and that I had an older sister, and that I left for Alexandria in 1933."

"And what about your father. Is he still alive?"

"He died four years ago, in 1961."

Dali blinked a moment, then glanced at the paper in front of him.

"Let's get back to the matter of religion," he said. "Is it correct, Cohn, that religion is a valuable thing?"

Elie nodded.

"So if someone says *Allah Akbar* (Allah is great), does that make him into a Moslem?"

"I don't know."

"But let me tell you something, Cohn," Dali said, raising his voice till it was like a roar of thunder. "Ever since you got the Talmud from your wise men and started to occupy your minds with it, you don't know what religion is and you're lost. God has led you astray because you've left the true religion, and taken hold of the Talmud.

"But the day will come when we'll get rid of that whole gang of yours, and all the agents together. There won't be any agent or spy left in the Arab homeland. We'll destroy all the agents to the last one. We'll finish you off at one blow." Dali gestured dramatically, and then added in a low voice, "Allah willing!"

Immediately thereafter the court orderly announced a break in the proceedings.

"The court will reconvene at three thirty P.M. to hear further testimony."

The crowd got up and a tumult broke out.

In the reporters' gallery the idea was prevalent that Dali would do everything to convict everyone who had cooperated with Elie Cohn. Their words showed a distinct tone of admiration for the man who had managed to hoodwink the top Syrian leadership.

13

The Trial—Second Phase

The next afternoon session of the court was devoted to investigating Eli Cohn's mission in Damascus.

The chief justice did not intend to neglect even the smallest detail out of all the facts and particulars, which were heard over and over again.

He especially wanted to denounce those newspapers and journalists who had come out with attacks on the Damascus regime and in defense of Elie Cohn.

"They're defending you," he claimed in rage, "because they're probably being paid for it."

"It could be," Elie replied placidly.

"What is your opinion of these papers and journalists?"

"They're all sold out; they're all agents."

"Like you?"

"No. I'm an envoy of my country. They're sold out and are doing it for money."

"You hear?" Dali cried from his judge's seat. "He's an envoy doing his duty while the others have sold out. Israel gets our oil royalties and pays these agents." Then the judge turned abruptly toward Elie. "Incidentally, what do you think about Israel?"

Elie hesitated for a moment before answering.

"I don't know," he said with a shrug of his shoulders. "In Egypt I was a good citizen, in Israel I don't know."

"But you must have some ideas about your country?" Dali insisted.

"I'd say that things are bad in Israel."

"And what do you think about the Radio Baghdad announcer who claims that you knew our whole leadership?"

Elie let out a deep sigh.

"I think he's crazy."

There were loud boos for Baghdad and for the accused in the courtroom. For ten minutes Dali banged the table with his wooden mallet, but quiet was not restored.

110

"The court!" he suddenly announced, banging the hammer on the side, "postpones its next session till tomorrow morning!"

Next morning, the courtroom was as packed as on the previous day. More so. Even the aisles were crowded with people waiting expectantly for the second session to begin.

Judge Dali sat motionless behind his desk while the jury entered in single file. After them, under heavy guard, came Elie Cohn and some thirty men and women accused of cooperation and espionage.

According to the complex Syrian rules and regulations, the trial was conducted by the chief justice. All the others were nothing but that colorful scenery so loved by the East.

The judge, who was also the investigator and the prosecutor, struck the desk sharply with his gavel. Silence reigned in the room. In the momentary stillness it was possible to hear the whirr of the television cameras and the whispered remarks of the reporters in the gallery.

Elie Cohn seemed more nervous that morning. Despite the strong desire to maintain the continuity of the trial and, naturally, to keep him alive until sentence was passed, it was clear that between one session and the next, the Syrians had been relentless in their persecution.

That the interrogations in the torture chambers of Camp 70 prison had broken him down completely was clearly evident in Elie's quivering profile on the television screens.

Elie ran one hand through his hair and mopped his forehead with the other.

Dali cleared his throat.

"In the course of yesterday's testimony," he said, "it became known that Elie Cohn did not only deal in espionage. He was also assigned to locate a Nazi by the name of Rosalie and to liquidate him in any way possible. Rosalie is dead. But who killed him?

"For the purpose of locating the Nazi, who was Eichmann's assistant, Elie made use of his friend Majd Sheikh El-Ard, a well-known merchant and businessman."

A roar of abuse rose in the courtroom, and the judge continued. "When the Eichmann trial was held in Jerusalem, the name of Rosalie emerged. Soon afterward Majd Sheikh El-Ard took Elie Cohn in his car to the quarter where the Nazi lived, and pointed out the house. Do you admit this fact, Majd?" Dali asked suddenly.

"I don't know what you're talking about, Your Honor,"
Majd claimed fervently.

"By Allah, you *do* know. What we want to know is how
many times you took Elie there."

"I don't know if I took him there even once."

"You don't remember, or you think you don't remember?"

"I don't remember, Your Honor, and I don't think."

Dali put it another way.

"Did you take Cohn there because you knew that Rosalie
himself was a German spy?"

"I didn't know that he was a spy at all."

"And what's this story about Springer?"

Majd shrugged his shoulders impatiently.

"That has nothing to do with it, Your Honor."

Dali frowned.

"Don't tell me what has to do with it. Tell me about this
Springer, whom we have yet to catch."

"Well, Springer was also a German, Your Honor. He used
to stay at the Hotel Omier every time he came to Damascus
on business. I met him at the El-Sharq Club and he introduced himself as an international businessman. I avoided having commercial ties with him, at least in the first phase."

"Why?"

Majd shrugged his shoulders.

"I don't know, Your Honor. I had the feeling that the man
wasn't a merchant but an agent of the Red Hand."

Dali smiled. The Red Hand was a French underground
movement which during the Algerian War operated in Europe and the Middle East, to sabotage arms supplies to the
rebels.

"Your suspicions are way off if you suspected an innocent
merchant, while Elie Cohn, who really *was* an enemy of the
State, you believed completely."

"That was something else, Your Honor. Cohn didn't look
like someone who was up to something. And anyway, if he
was accepted in the top leadership, why shouldn't I accept
him? I'm a Syrian patriot, aren't I?"

A murmur passed through the courtroom and the judge
rapped his gavel twice.

"Let's not talk about your patriotic contribution to the
State, Sheikh El-Ard. I want to ask you if it ever occurred to
you that both Cohn and Springer are not, let's say, positive
types. Especially in view of the fact that both of them are
foreign elements?"

"I don't know, Your Honor. I am a merchant and these people had commercial relations with me and nothing else. How could I know that they were spies?"

Dali gave a grunt of disappointment, but wasn't ready to give up his prey.

"Let's leave Springer for now. Tell us why you took Elie to Rosalie."

"I've already told you that I never took Cohn to see Rosalie, Your Honor."

"Cohn!" The chief justice turned to Elie. "Tell us the truth. Was Majd with you at Rosalie's, or did you get there with the help of Allah?"

Elie Cohn lowered his eyes to the courtroom all around and nodded.

"Speak louder, Cohn," one of the judges barked. "So Majd can also hear the truth."

"I maintain that it was Majd Sheikh El-Ard who brought me to Rosalie's residence. He volunteered to do it one evening when I came to him. He pointed out a house in Shahabander Street, not far from the Central Bank."

Majd turned white. His face trembled and his hands were clenched.

"Your Honor, the accused's words are taken out of thin air!" he cried emotionally.

"*Your* story is taken from thin air! You're a liar!"

"No! By the life of Allah, I'm not!"

"You took Cohn to Rosalie. You took him there!"

Majd spread his arms dramatically.

"Believe me, Your Honor, it's all a lie. I am an old and honorable man. Why shouldn't you believe me?"

"If we believe you that you didn't take Cohn to Rosalie, can you tell me how you came to talk about this man with Cohn, or to arrange a meeting between the two?"

Majd buried his face in his hands.

"I don't remember."

"Did you know who Rosalie was?" Dali asked him.

"Of course. I knew that he was a German, and that during the Second World War he was Eichmann's assistant in the Jewish Section."

"And it never occurred to you that Rosalie might be a spy?"

"No, why should I think that, Your Honor?" Majd wondered. "Is Syria completely riddled with agents and spies?"

For a long moment there was silence in the courtroom.

Dali consulted with two of his assistants. Then he renewed his barrage of questions.

The idea in the foreign correspondents' gallery was that Majd had become Dali's daily victim. He wouldn't let him go till he had wrung the last drop of blood out of the elderly merchant.

"Did you ever hear the name Von Hantke. Majd El-Ard?"

"I've heard of him. He was head of the Arab Department in the German Foreign Office during the Nazi regime. Two or three years ago he went to Riyadh and we read in the papers that he had been appointed government adviser in Saudi Arabia."

"Did you know that he was a Jew-lover, and that after the war every time the problem of the Jews came up, he used to take a positive stand?"

"He may have done that after the war. But as I remember him from my contacts with that same institution, he was a Jew-hater."

"Okay," Dali sighed. "Let's get back to the business of Rosalie."

He turned to Elie Cohn.

"What was the reason that one bright day you decided to get on Rosalie's trail? Did they tell you to do it?"

Elie nodded.

"In a telegram?"

"Yes, in a telegram."

"When did it reach you?"

"A short time after the opening of the Eichmann trial," Elie said.

"What did the Israelis want from Rosalie?"

"It was found that he had been responsible for the destruction of a considerable number of Jews, and it was decided to assassinate him. When I got the telegram, I turned to my friend Majd and asked him about Rosalie. He led me to him."

Majd yelled in rage, "Your Honor! He's lying! He's accusing me falsely. Is there no way of pressuring him into telling the truth?"

Dali smiled with diabolical glee.

"There's no need to pressure Cohn. When he tells the truth, you can hear it plainly."

14

The Trial—Conclusion

The session of the special court that reconvened in the afternoon dealt with investigating the part played by Salem Saif, the Radio Damascus announcer who was one of Elie Cohn's friends and had even helped him obtain information.

A murmur was heard in the courtroom when Salem Saif was summoned to be questioned. An attractive-looking man with a roundish face and a genial, decent expression, he quickly got to his feet and looked at the panel of judges.

"Are you Salem Saif, foreign news editor of Radio Damascus?"

"Yes, sir."

"In the course of the investigation of the chief accused, your name was included in a conspicuous and central manner in the information we obtained. You helped Elie Cohn obtain valuable information from prime sources which were intended for you, and you alone, in the framework of your function as editor of the news department. Have you anything to say against the accusation?"

The courtroom was absolutely silent.

"No, sir."

Dali wrinkled his forehead and consulted with his deputy.

The answer had surprised him somewhat.

"Again, Salem Saif," he said, "do you admit to the charge without appeal?"

"No, sir," Salem said. "I very much fear that the court has not properly investigated and understood the words of the chief accused. My version admits the final outcome of the case, but not the way in which you arrived at it."

"Do you imagine, Mr. Intellectual," Dali said with mocking irony, "that legal philosophizing will change anything?"

"I don't know how it is in military trials, but in civil courts they take into account extenuating circumstances."

Dali compressed his lips until they turned pale.

"This is not a military trial, Saif, and it's better if you stop

115

jabbering in that direction. The trial taking place here is a public trial, seen by millions on the television screens, and it will be written up in all the newspapers."

Salem chuckled out loud.

"I have no doubt that it will be televised and written about. But don't tell me, Your Honor, what will be the role of Colonel Bakri, the Chief Censor, in all this."

For a moment there was an uproar in the courtroom, and then a feeling of dismay. Dali rose and struck the desk as rage overwhelmed him.

"Salem Saif, you are accused here of cooperating with a foreign element. We are prepared to overlook your last remark against this public trial. But I must warn you that any more remarks of this sort will result in your being tried for contempt of court."

Salem nodded.

"What do you want to hear from me that you haven't yet milked from the chief accused?"

"How did you get to Elie?"

"Friends of mine suggested that I get together with him, and when I did, I discovered that he was a very pleasant chap."

"And that's why you decided to let him in on your secret work?"

"There was no secrecy involved in my work."

"But you got valuable information from the Ministry of Information, in order to take out suitable extracts. The fact that this material was given for classification shows how valuable it was."

"Not necessarily," Salem protested. "A large part of it was a printed agglomeration of long, unimportant speeches by members of the government, where I had to take out the interesting essence."

"Was it hard work?" Dali asked.

"No, not especially."

"Then why did you bring Cohn into it?"

"Cohn gave the impression of being a patriot, a man close to the top leadership, and an intellectual. I never for a moment imagined that I was compromising myself in cooperating with him."

"You lie, Salem!" Dali yelled angrily. "I've never seen such a liar. Your dramatic appearance and careful choice of words cover up a mountain of lies. This court knows that you were

Cohn's contact man here in Damascus, even before he had set foot on Syrian soil."

Salem shuddered.

"You're mistaken. There must have been some slipup in the investigation. I've already told you how I met Cohn."

"Cohn told us that when he went to Argentina in 1963, in order to open a campaign there on behalf of the Baath, you wrote to him and asked him to send you the key to his apartment. Do you admit that Salem Saif?"

"Yes, Your Honor."

"Why did you do that?"

"I wanted to use his apartment to hold rendezvous with girls without my wife's knowledge," Saif said.

The courtroom buzzed.

"And not in order to broadcast information to Israel in Cohn's place?" Dali asked in a voice that was close to a scream.

"No!" Saif cried. "No, I swear it by Allah!"

The chief justice turned to Elie Cohn and gave him an inquisitive look.

"How is it that you let Saif do whatever he wanted in your apartment?" he asked. "Weren't you afraid he'd discover the transmitting equipment and turn you in?"

Cohn looked at Salem Saif and said, "From my knowledge of Saif, I was convinced that even if he had discovered that I was a spy, he wouldn't have turned me in. Saif and I had an arrangement between us. When I left Damascus on one of my trips, I'd leave the key to the apartment in my mailbox. Saif had another key to the mailbox."

"Is that right, Saif?" Colonel Dali asked.

Salem Saif nodded.

"Tell me, Saif, did you know or suspect that Kamel Amin Tabet wasn't an emigrant from Argentina?"

"Why should I have suspected?"

"Because they told you here or outside to contact him and to give him as much information as you could."

"I'm afraid I know very well what you're getting at, Your Honor, but I must hold to the truth."

The judge appeared to be reaching the end of his patience. He cried fervently:

"My brothers the judges, gentlemen of the audience, is it not impertinence for the accused to stick to his story, when even a deaf man can tell he is lying?"

He paused for a moment, then continued: "The court has

heard your version and the extenuating circumstances. Do you admit though that in the years you knew Cohn you passed on at least a number of items of information of security value?"

"Probably," Salem said. "But I didn't do it before I knew that Kamel-Cohn was getting information, and enjoying prefferential civil rights from the administration itself."

Dali suddenly looked at the accused.

"Were you not the person who pushed Cohn into high society here in Damascus?"

"No, sir," Salem objected. "Kamel came to Damascus with an abundance of recommendations, thanks to his acquaintance with the President himself."

"As an intelligent man, Salem Saif, I am perplexed how a recommendation or a chance acquaintance with a general at a garden party can influence your logical reason, especially in view of the fact that the work was, at least in part, of a security nature."

Salem raised his head and stared straight at the judge.

"I was not the only one who erred in connection with Cohn. All Damascus could appear here in the prisoner's dock."

Dali called for the remark to be removed from the record.

There was a moment of silence, followed by reflection and consultations. Then the judge asked, "When Eli Cohn returned to Israel the last time, shortly after the famous border incident, you were the first man to talk to him?"

"Yes, is there anything wrong in that?"

"Were you not sent by someone to hint to Elie that things weren't as they used to be?"

Salem shrugged.

"No one sent me. Anyway, Elie Cohn was smart enough to understand the situation. It was the top leadership which made him suspect a change. How could you expect him not to feel it?"

"Thank you, Salem. Your evidence, for today, is concluded. We'll return to you in the course of the trial."

Salem gave a sigh of relief and sat down.

The procedure in Syrian military courts is different from that of other courts of its type elsewhere.

The chief justice in a Syrian military court does not merely listen and judge, but conducts investigations himself, poses questions, and passes remarks.

The testimony procedures are also peculiar to the Syrian Law. The accused does not take the witness stand to give his testimony, but testifies from his place in the prisoner's dock. The chief justice interrupts him from time to time by posing questions to the other prisoners.

This procedure resulted in a certain amount of confusion in reports of the trial and made it difficult to follow its course consecutively. An additional difficulty was the fact that whole sections of the trial were not permitted to be published in Damascus—among them the entire second session of the court.

For that reason, when, in the fourth session of the trial, a hint came up of the presence of another Israeli spy, there was no reference to it in the records of the previous sessions.

The Lebanese paper *Al Hiyyat* reported, by way of introduction, to the fourth session:

"In the sensational trial of Elie Cohn, the Israeli spy, it was revealed that an additional Jewish spy is hiding in Syria. It turned out that Cohn received a telegram from Israel containing instructions to search out the whereabouts of the Israeli spy, who it was feared had been arrested. The designation of the man in the telegram from Israel was The Unknown.

The president of the court, Colonel Sallah Dali, opened the paper, read it solemnly, and then looked at Elie Cohn.

"Tell me, Cohn," he said in a thundering voice, "who is the spy that you call The Unknown?"

Elie hesitated a moment before answering.

"He's an Israeli spy who operated in Syria and with whom contact has been lost."

"What's his name?"

"I don't know."

"You're lying!" Dali yelled.

"I don't know and I didn't even ask the center in Tel Aviv," Elie said placidly.

Colonel Dali frowned.

"And they asked you to renew contact with him?"

"They wanted me to find out whether he was being held in Maza or Tadmor Prison."

"And what did you find out?" the chief justice asked.

"I didn't succeed in tracing him," Elie admitted. "I reported that to Tel Aviv."

Colonel Dali glanced at the charge sheet in front of him.

"Now, Cohn, tell the court what your connections were with Lieutenant Ma'azi Zaher a-Din."

Elie Cohn turned his head to the left and noted the pale face of the moustachioed lieutenant. His head was bowed and his lips trembled.

"In June, 1962," Elie began, "I went to Beirut, and from there, via Europe, to Israel. I informed the Center that I had managed to make friends with an officer by the name of Ma'azi Zaher a-Din. They ordered me to tighten my contacts with him."

Cohn hesitated only for a second.

"When he was appointed area commander of Badlev," he went on, "I went to visit him, and when he came to Damascus he used to stay with me. Once he noticed an unusual radio antenna at my place. I explained to him that it was an antenna enabling me to pick up Buenos Aires. He nodded and didn't say a word.

"I obtained the most important military information when I joined Ma'azi on a tour of the army center at El-Hama. He pointed out the location of important positions, and I passed this information on to Israel. On one of my visits I was invited to his office, where I saw a map of the area of Kuneitra. He showed me where the fortifications were to be built."

"Do you admit to all that, Lieutenant Ma'azi?" Colonel Dali barked.

The lieutenant blinked in confusion and mumbled something under his moustache.

"Speak louder, you dog!" Dali roared.

Ma'azi glanced at the hostile crowd and said, "It's true that I toured the region of El-Hama with Cohn. It's true that he asked me about all sorts of army installations we passed on the way. But I didn't answer him."

"And what about the map of Kuneitra?" the chief justice interrupted him. "Why did you show him where the fortifications were about to be built?"

"He told me that he was thinking of buying land in the area," Lieutenant Ma'azi explained. "And so I pointed out the plots that the army was going to appropriate for the installations."

"And what else?"

"He wanted to photograph the map."

"And you let him do it?" Dali burst out.

"No, I didn't. It was a military map, and Cohn, after all, was a civilian."

"You're lying!"

"He isn't lying. I didn't photograph the map."

Elie Cohn's placid voice struck Colonel Dali dumb. He glared at Elie and mumbled something unintelligible. Then he turned to the perplexed lieutenant.

"Tell us a bit about your visits to Elie Cohn's apartment," he ordered.

"We were good friends, like two brothers," Lieutenant Ma'azi related. "I stayed at his house often and one thing amazed me. Five out of the seven rooms in the apartment weren't in use at all. Besides that, I didn't understand why Cohn, who spent money on all kinds of causes, refused to hire a maid, and cleaned the house, washed the dishes, and cooked his meals all by himself."

"And you didn't suspect a thing?" Dali sneered. "A citizen who lives on a high level, spends money without working, pays a fortune for a giant apartment, and uses only two rooms! You knew all this and didn't even suspect that something was wrong!"

"I didn't suspect, Your Honor," Ma'azi mumbled. "Apparently, I'm not too clever at making deductions."

"You're not clever at anything, except betrayal of the Fatherland, Lieutenant Ma'azi!" Colonel Dali roared.

In the course of the testimony, it was learned that the head of Syrian Intelligence, Colonel Swidani, was full of admiration for Elie Cohn's work. Swidani told how Elie's home had served as a meeting place for persons of high society and how Elie himself showed considerable knowledge in many fields such as politics, commerce, military life, and social activity.

"Trailing Elie Cohn," the colonel told the judge, "was a hard job. The man," he said, pointing to the accused, "acted with great circumspection. He didn't keep a maid, a chauffeur, or a cook. He did everything himself, washed the dishes, cleaned the apartment, and even did the laundry. Not only that, he was careful not to meet the same man twice in one day. With special visitors he instituted a system of special rings on the doorbell."

The colonel sighed for a moment, then continued: "After we had located the source of the broadcasts, we planned the invasion of his apartment for eight A.M., on the assumption that at that hour he would still be in bed. The break-in was planned in such a way that he wouldn't be able to resist, or even commit suicide by jumping out the window. Three trained security men were ordered to burst into the bedroom. One of them was given the job of flattening himself on Elie. The whole operation was supposed to be over in less than five minutes."

"And when you broke in as planned," Dali said, "did you find Elie in bed?"

"No. He was already up. We caught him red-handed—that is, while he was actually broadcasting. Things like this happen to people like me only once or twice in a lifetime."

"Did he try to resist arrest?"

"He said that his name was Kamel Amin Tabet, and repeated it several times. Later he broke down and confessed that his name was Elie Cohn, and that he was working for the Israeli espionage service. Beside his bed we found an announcement that had been received by radio from Tel Aviv; in it, Elie was requested to provide more information on a certain member of the government."

"Apart from that, did you find any other incriminating documents in the apartment?"

Swidani grinned, showing yellow teeth.

"We carried out a careful search and found recorded tapes that were to be sent to Israel, disappearing ink, fingers of gelatine, Swiss checkbooks, and other equipment for spying."

Dali surveyed the audience filling the hall to capacity, then tossed out his question cunningly.

"For a security man like you, Ahmed Swidani, what is the significance of these findings?"

"These are primary accessories of a spy, Your Honor," he said, still grinning. "And Elie is a first-rate spy."

And then, when all eyes were turned to the Israeli spy, Swidani spread his hands in a theatrical gesture and said fervently, "Israel is the devil, and Cohn is the devil's advocate!"

Jamer felt his body cover with sweat as he looked in the direction in which Muhi Ibrahim was pointing and saw the solid figure of Sallah Dali, who had risen in order to make his concluding speech and deliver his verdict.

Dali's face was tense and slightly flushed. He stuck out his tongue, moistened his thick lips, and looked at the crowd which was waiting for his words with holy awe.

The verdict had been handed down a week before, but had not yet been published, due to pressure from higher authorities. That morning it had been decided to announce the results to all.

"My brothers the Arabs, and citizens of Damascus," Dali began, "this special court has heard for the past two months the exploits of the Israeli agent Elie Cohn, who masqueraded as a rich Moslem by the name of Kamel Amin Tabet. The facts have all spoken against him, and the accused has not tried to deny them. Since there is no need to speak at length on this regrettable affair, I will read the verdict as recorded in the protocol of this court:

"Whereas the evidence and facts that were submitted to this court have persuaded it beyond all shadow of doubt, that the accused Eliyahu Ben Shaul Cohn, alias Kamel Amin Tabet, infiltrated the El'al area, which is a military area to which entry is forbidden, for the purpose of obtaining information liable to be of use to the enemy;

"And whereas the act of entry into the area is subject to the death penalty under Sections 158 and 159 of the Military Tribunal Constitution;

"And whereas this information is liable to be of assistance to the enemy, it must remain secret for reasons of State security, the one responsible for obtaining such information is sentenced to death under Sections 271, 272, and 234 of the Military Tribunal Constitution.

"In the name of the special Tribunal,

"Colonel Sallah Dali"

The chief justice sat down again.

The courtroom was in a turmoil. Cries of encouragement, rage, and bitterness blended into a screeching chorus. In the press gallery there was total silence, while in the prisoner's dock the condemned man continued to stand at attention, dumb.

"Look carefully at what's happening," Muhi Ibrahim remarked. "This is the face of Damascus of the Baath."

Jamer turned on him.

"Shut your mouth, Muhi. You're in the middle of Damascus, and the walls have ears."

"Yes. Last month, two Americans. This month, Elie Cohn. The crowd is thirsty for blood, and the regime is giving them enough to get drunk on."

Nonidentification with the judges' decision wasn't the exclu-

sive lot of Jamer and Muhi Ibrahim, the exclusive correspondents of the Lebanese paper *Al-Asbua*, who had been,
sent to cover the trial. A tone of dissatisfaction was also
reflected in the articles of the news agency writers and most
of the foreign papers.

The Damascus regime was careful in selecting the reporters
who were invited to cover the trial. But it couldn't prevent
them from admiring and sympathizing with the Israeli agent
for what he had achieved.

In the courtroom, crowds still remained cheering the
court's decision. Muhi stood there for a long while, in amazement.

"It's one o'clock," Jamer remarked, looking at his watch.
"It's time to go get something to eat."

"How can you even think of it?"

Jamer shrugged his shoulders indifferently.

"I think that the outcome was clear from the beginning.
I'm not too surprised. I've gotten used to the idea that one
day it would happen, and that day has come."

"No, it wouldn't have come," Ibrahim protested. "World
public opinion was too strong and the decision to execute Elie
Cohn stemmed perhaps from a desire for personal revenge
rather than legal justice."

Jamer shrugged.

"I think that's something for the historians to argue about.
What's clear is that it was impossible to leave Cohn just like
that, after two Americans whose guilt was a whole lot less
were hanged last month."

He watched Muhi's reaction.

"Shall we go have something to eat?"

In the Ali Restaurant up the street, there was a brief debate between local journalists and two foreign correspondents. The general opinion was that this outcome was expected
from the first moment.

"What Dali did today," one of the reporters remarked,
"was a cheap matinee performance. Lots of drama and
cruelty."

"I think I'll leave for Lebanon today," Muhi said. "This
place is making me sick."

"They shouldn't have sent you here," a local reporter said
brusquely. "This is no place for someone with a weak
stomach."

15

Appeals, Appeals

From the moment the sentence was officially published, the great Israeli propaganda machine all over the world went into high gear.

The Foreign Office and Israeli embassies abroad mobilized all their connections with high-ranking persons all over the world, and from the petitions submitted by various personages and organizations, it turned out that there had been no case in the past ten years that had aroused their consciences on behalf of a cause as much as the Elie Cohn affair.

Pope Paul the Sixth sent a personal note to the Syrian President and in its wake came comments by a number of Arab cardinals who had been elevated to their exalted positions only a few weeks before by the Pope himself.

The secular authorities in Italy were not far behind. Personalities of the highest echelons, including the ex-mayor of Florence, Georgio La Fira, appealed personally to the head of the Syrian Revolutionary Council, Amin El-Hafez, with a request for clemency for Elie Cohn.

The main activity, however, was concentrated in neighboring France. Two former premiers, Antoine Pinay and Edgar Faure, intervened more than once on Elie's behalf.

In Paris, scores of senators were mobilized for a propaganda campaign of hitherto unheard-of proportions. Elie Cohn's two attorneys—the president of the Barrister's Association, Paul Arrighi, and Jacques Mercier—submitted in the name of Nadia Cohn a request to General de Gaulle to use his influence on General El-Hafez to nullify the decree.

From Belgium came the emotional appeal of the Queen Mother Elisabeth to the head of the Syrian Revolutionary Council—an appeal that fell on deaf ears.

Ex-Premier of Belgium Camille Huysmans expressed readiness to go to Damascus personally to intervene in the matter.

Twenty-two British Members of Parliament—including many pro-Arabs—sent a petition for a retrial.

In the United States, the heads of the Syrian and Lebanese communities expressed their nonidentification with the sentence.

From Canada came an appeal by former Prime Minister John Diefenbaker.

In the Scandinavian and Benelux countries, members of Parliament, journalists, scientists, and men of letters joined the cause, as well as various organizations such as the International Red Cross, the League for the Protection of Human Rights, and the International Association of Jurists.

On March 8, a week after the broadcast of the trial had begun, the Swedish branch of Amnesty International sent a telegram to the President of Syria requesting clemency for Elie Cohn. The cable read:

> *Cohn is not a Syrian citizen. And in civilized countries foreign espionage agents are not executed. There has not been one case where Syrian spies convicted in Israel were executed.*

No reply to this cable was received.

On March 27, the Foreign Minister of Argentina, Dr. Miguel Angel Zabala Ortez, announced that he had appealed to the Syrian Government to reprieve the sentence of Elie Cohn, who was a citizen of Argentina. His request was submitted for humanitarian reasons, and in view of the fact that Argentina did not have the death penalty.

At the same time, Dr. Ortez revealed that an additional request for clemency had been submitted—for a woman citizen of Argentina who had been sentenced to death in Damascus on charges of espionage on behalf of Israel. The Argentine Foreign Minister refused to divulge her name or whether she was one of those who had been tried with Elie Cohn.

Especally moving was the appeal of another Argentinian, Cardinal Pelcius. The Cardinal was on his deathbed, and a few moments before he passed away he formulated his request to General Amin El-Hafez, in which he stated explicitly that this was in the nature of his last will and testament.

The Cardinal's request was nevertheless denied.

Meanwhile, Jacques Mercier, Cohn's attorney, was knocking incessantly on the doors of all the Damascus ministries. After much effort he managed to get a short interview with Colonel Swidani, head of Syrian Intelligence.

"Do you think," Mercier asked, trying to play on his self-esteem, "that El-Hafez, out of esteem for you, wouldn't respond to the request?"

"I'm certain he wouldn't. He's worked himself into such a state that nobody can tell him what to do. Kamel was his good friend, yet nothing can stop him from executing him. Even Doctor Quiss, who saved his life and whom Hafez promised before he left Paris that he would pay back some-day—sent a request for clemency. Hafez didn't even bother to reply."

Mercier gave a deep sigh.

"It may be," he said in a low voice, "that your President is a man without human feelings. Do you think you might be able to interest him in the special offer I'm bringing on behalf of the Israeli Government?"

The colonel reflected a moment.

"I'm wondering what the Israeli Government could offer in exchange for Cohn's life."

He sighed.

"It's clear to you that the offer to release ten Syrian spies in exchange for Elie Cohn is not sufficient. The ten men that Israel wants to exchange for Elie are finished."

"Like Elie Cohn," Mercier said.

"No. Elie is an Israeli national hero. In spite of everything, we don't know what he managed to find out about Syria, and what information he passed on during his years of operation. He's still hot, even now after he's been condemned."

Mercier nodded.

"The Israeli Government has thought about this possibility. They offer you medical aid, spare auto parts and jeeps, and military supplies."

Mercier studied Swidani's expression.

"Is the present offer more realistic?" he asked.

"Well, it would be excellent in any other case. However—"

"Why isn't it good in Elie Cohn's case?"

"Because it would look silly," Swidani said. "El-Hafez and the Syrian Government do not recognize the Zionist state. How can they trade with it? Don't you see that such a deal would be an indirect form of recognition?"

Mercier laughed.

"But that's silly. You won't gain a thing by Elie's death. On the other hand, you can gain equipment worth millions, as well as favorable world public opinion."

Swidani thought for a moment.

"The deal itself may interest El-Hafez," he said. "But don't think I'd mention public opinion."

"In any case," Mercier said, "make him the offer. No one has to publicize the deal. It'll be carried out behind the scenes."

"Of course. No one thought for a moment to make bally-hoo out of this," Swidani said. "Call me in two days. I assume that I'll have an answer by then."

On Monday morning, Mercier again knocked on Swidani's door. The colonel wasn't in, but his aide received him and told him El-Hafez' decision.

"The answer is a decided No," the man said. "El-Hafez is not prepared for any deals. And he seems to know what he's doing."

Mercier ran his fingers nervously through his hair.

"Is there no chance of my seeing the President?"

"I'm afraid not, sir," the aide said. "But if you haven't yet given up, try to pressure Judge Dali. He has a certain amount of influence on El-Hafez."

Mercier extended his hand in thanks.

"Mr. Mercier," the aide said, "I admire a man who doesn't give up in a hurry. It seems what Swidani has said and El-Hafez' decision have not yet brought you to despair. You have impenetrable armor, Mercier."

The attorney nodded.

"Give my thanks to Swidani for his efforts. I'll know how to appreciate them if the situation changes for the better."

That same afternoon, another important visitor was waiting for Swidani.

"Colonel," the lieutenant said. "You have a visitor from *Al Usbua al-Arbi.*"

"That arrogant reporter?" Swidani grumbled. "I hope that he doesn't have the impudence to ask for clemency in the name of the Arab world?"

"No. He wants to see you without delay."

"What's his name?"

"Hasanin."

Swidani nodded lazily.

"He used to be close to the regime, and now he defends its opponents. Tell him to come in."

Hasanin, tall, with bony face and deep-set eyes, came in with rapid steps.

"My name's Hasanin," he said, extending his hand. "I assume you've already heard of me and of the newspaper I'm representing in the Cohn affair."

"Unfortunately, your articles have been the subject of several conversations among myself, the President, and the chief justice," Swidani said, without hiding his hostility. "I don't know how to formulate the question, but tell me, is there an organization supporting your paper, so that it will support opponents of the regime?"

"I very much fear, sir," Hasanin said with studied calm, "that you aren't acquainted with our weekly. It was pro-Baath when the Baath was still the party of the masses. Now, when the ideas are running out and the nation is turning its back, the Baath is trying to grab onto Elie Cohn or a couple of wretched American agents."

Swidani made a face of disgust.

"One has to be as impudent as you are in order to say before a representative of the regime what you have just said," he snapped. "And now, tell me what's the urgency in this meeting with me?"

"I'd like to interview Elie Cohn in his cell."

Swidani raised his eyebrows in amazement.

"I've never heard anything so silly."

"It's not silly. It's very likely that in speaking with Cohn, I'll find points in favor of the regime. Besides, I'm not in the habit of writing commentary. All I do is report what I see."

Swidani reflected for a moment.

"Very well. You can have ten minutes with him. A security officer will be present throughout, and your article will pass through censorship before being sent to Lebanon."

The meeting in Elie's cell took place the next day.

Hasanin was given ten minutes with the prisoner.

"When you set out on your mission to Damascus, did you know you were putting a rope around your neck?"

"In my subconscious I knew I was taking a risk," Elie replied. "But like every man, I believed I had a chance of succeeding. In any case, I took the assignment to ensure the future of my wife, my mother, and my three children. It was only for their sakes that I agreed to take on this risky mission."

Hasanin scrutinized Elie's face, but saw no change.

"From the trial I learned that when you were close to the top leadership, and a member of the Baath, you contributed considerable sums of money to the party and affiliated bodies.

These contributions helped in the procurement of weapons and the establishment of the regime's position. Don't you think that you may have exaggerated playing the role of a Syrian patriot to the point where you might have been looked on as a traitor in your own country?"

Elie looked up angrily.

"No, I did not betray my country. I knew exactly what I was doing and they trusted me completely I couldn't have got where I did if it hadn't been for these investments."

"You said before that you believed you could get out of any spot. What made you think so?"

"My assignment was to end on our Independence Day, at the beginning of next May."

Hasanin wanted to ask more questions, but the security officer told him to finish up.

"The ten minutes are up, Mr. Journalist."

Hasanin pressed Elie's hand and whispered, "I want you to know that I and my colleagues admire you."

16

The Execution of Elie Cohn

Mercier sat in complete silence and surveyed the decorations on the wall of the room. Dali came in. His mood was grim.

"Haven't we met before, Mr. Advocate?" he asked.

"Indeed, yes. And I fear that the matter becomes much more urgent today, in the light of the sentence you have passed."

"Have you anything against the sentence, Advocate?" Dali asked in a mocking tone.

Mercier hesitated.

"To tell you the truth, you haven't adhered to all the minutiae of legal propriety. However, as you will understand, I haven't come here to split hairs. I want to prevent the execution of the prisoner."

Dali was so furious that the words stuck in his throat. Finally he managed to gain control of himself.

"Now," he said in a frozen voice, "I am forced to request you to leave. You don't know what you're asking. I am certain that you don't realize what might happen if we did not sentence him to death. Have you thought of the repercussions?"

"When you speak of repercussions, why don't you take account of the negative repercussions of this affair abroad? Have you never thought of something known as public opinion?"

Dali did not take the trouble to answer. But his expression of fear showed that even the judge was not content with the sentence.

"The big mistake of the country that sent you," he said, "is that it's capable of mobilizing world opinion in this matter. This would undermine the regime's ego—an ego that must *not* lose face in the eyes of the electors. It must be independent and free of external influence. The Elie Cohn affair has grown to the point that the top leadership is uneasy. I am very doubtful if all Israel's efforts will manage to gain him clemency."

"However—"

Dali looked at Mercier with controlled rage.

"It's better that we leave this question. The Head of State has already ratified the sentence."

"But you have the right to give him a retrial, and to enable him to appeal to the institutions of justice, or at least to meet with a lawyer, who will tell him of the efforts being made to save him."

Dali got up and went over to the door.

"You may leave now, Mercier. You've done your work, and I don't want to hear another word on this subject."

Mercier got up and left. After months of incessant running around, months of mobilizing every spiritual and material resource for the rescue of Elie Cohn, Mercier was badly hurt by the way in which he had been received by Dali, and the humiliating manner in which he had been dismissed.

He knew that the execution was only a matter of days, or perhaps hours, away.

For a moment his heart was pinched by the thought that his letter to Elie had not been received. There was no doubt that in Elie's heart the thought lurked that in his last days he had been deserted by his friends and country.

Mercier went out, hailed a cab, and drove to the Samara Hotel, where he had stayed for two disappointing and depressing months.

With shaking knees he climbed up to his room, sat down heavily behind his desk, took out writing paper and began to write.

March 3, 1965

His Excellency
Walid Talb
Minister of the Presidium

Your Excellency,

Please bring the contents of this letter to the knowledge of General Amin El-Hafez, and the President of the court, which is now trying Cohn in Damascus.

I arrived in Damascus on January 26, after Arrighi and myself were appointed counsel for the defense of Elie Cohn. The next day you agreed to receive me at

4:30 P.M. at the Presidential Palace. In that conversation, which took place in the presence of the General Secretary of the Presidium, Mamoun al-Attasi, who served as interpreter, you made the following declaration to me:

1. The police investigation had not yet been completed and so it was not yet possible to contact the accused. On the other hand, the moment the case was brought before a military tribunal, the counsel for the defense would be permitted to visit the accused and assure his defense.

2. You stressed that after receipt of confirmation, I would be permitted to appear in court.

3. The moment the police investigation was concluded, you would inform us by wire.

4. You agreed to transmit to the accused a letter, in which we informed him that we were his counsel.

I thanked you for this declaration in a letter from Paris, dated February 4th, 1965. From that day to this, a month's time, I have received no information on this affair.

Therefore, in the light of the reports which appeared in the press that the trial had begun, I decided to return to Damascus. The Secretary of the Presidium received me gladly on Saturday, February 26, at 5:30 P.M. at Mohajorin Palace. He declared before me that there had been no developments since our last meeting, when I had received your promises.

Therefore I was greatly astonished to learn the next evening, that the trial of Elie Cohn had begun. Not only did you not inform me of the conclusion of the investigation, but at the very time that I was in Damascus, I was not given the opportunity to defend Elie Cohn.

Therefore I immediately requested a meeting with you, Your Excellency, on Monday, March 1st. We met that day at 10:30 A.M. in the Presidential Palace, in the presence of Mamoun al-Attasi.

I expressed my sharp protests at your failure to honor your promises. At the same time, in reply to the request that I had submitted to General Amin El-Hafez to meet with Cohn, you informed me that I could meet him that same day. Your Excellency added that you would probably permit me to be present in the courtroom as an observer, together with al-Attasi as interpreter.

However, in the light of these statements, according to which you denied defense to the accused, I informed you that I would give you my answer after talking with the accused. I returned to my hotel, where al-Attasi was to telephone me at noon the same day, to inform me when I could meet with Elie Cohn.

An hour after the appointed time, al-Attasi called and informed me that the military tribunal had decided unanimously not to permit me to meet with Elie Cohn, and that this was a final decision, with no possibility of appeal.

Thus again the Syrian authorities broke their promise. Is this an example of justice in the Revolutionary Regime?—I ask.

You have broken all your promises.

I protest to the Syrian Government on this offense against all law and morality.

Jacques Mercier
Advocate

His hand shook with anger, as he signed his name to the letter. Then he folded it and slowly inserted it into a long envelope.

For a moment, as he licked the envelope, he was doubtful if the letter would reach its destination. But it was his duty to put down in writing the iniquity done to Elie Cohn.

His head buzzed like a hornet's nest, and shivers ran up and down his spine. Suddenly he saw before his eyes the agonized figure of Nadia, holding the children of her marriage with Elie.

At Maza airport, near Damascus, a correspondent for one of the news agencies buttonholed him and showered him with questions. But Mercier paid no heed.

The only words he said were, "Syria has disappointed me. I have nothing to add."

Later that same night, a cable arrived at his office in Paris.

Elie Cohn (it read) *will be hanged tomorrow morning.*

He looked at the words and everything grew foggy before his eyes. Though his mission had been important and he had done much in the attempt to save Elie Cohn, Mercier felt that he had failed. He lifted the receiver, dialed his partner Le Grand, and broke the news in a dry voice.

"Hanging him, just like that?" Le Grand said.

"Hanging him, just like that," Mercier repeated and hung-up.

His next call was to the Israeli Embassy. The Ambassador answered.

Mercier notified him sadly.

"We did everything possible. I must inform you and your government that I appreciate all that you did and your good-will. Unfortunately, you did not negotiate with the right party. Because in spite of everything, Elie will be hanged to-night after midnight, in the city square, the place where the two Americans were hanged two months ago."

On the other end there was a heavy silence.

The connection was broken silently.

Shortly after midnight, a police armored car, escorted by an army truckload of armed soldiers, arrived at the gates of Maza Prison in Damascus.

The jailers sitting beside the gate opened the door before the police car and it glided inside to the prison yard. The army truck remained outside, with all its soldiers deployed along the wall for security.

Dim voices were heard in the stillness of the night, and the creaking of door hinges and the rattle of chains. Then the door of the armored car was shut and slowly it slipped out of the prison yard.

The next moment the two cars were on their way to the police station near Al-Marjha Square, in the center of the city.

At the police station, in a closed cell, Elie was given his last privilege.

"Is there any debt or money that you'd like to leave anyone?" Judge Dali asked. He had arrived that evening to attend the execution.

"I don't owe anything to anyone. I have nothing to give," Elie said.

"Have you any last request?"

"I'd like to write to my wife and children. And I'd like to see a Jewish Rabbi to pray before I die."

Dali approved the request.

With trembling hands, a few moments before he mounted the scaffold, Elie wrote to his wife.

My beloved Nadia
My beloved family!

I am writing these last words to you in the hope that you will always stay together. I ask my wife to forgive me, to take care of herself, and to give our children a good education . . . The day will come when they will be proud of me.

And to you, my dear Nadia. You are free to marry another man, to give our children a father. In this matter you are completely free. I ask you not to mourn what happened, but to look to the future.

I am sending you last kisses.

Pray for my soul.

Elie

Immediately after the signing of the letter, which was deposited with Dali, the Chief Rabbi of Damascus, Rabbi Nissim Andabu, was permitted to be alone with the condemned man.

Twenty minutes later the rabbi was led out of the room, tears in his eyes.

Elie Cohn was dressed in a bright white gown inscribed in black chalk:

ELIE COHN
CONDEMNED TO DIE BY HANGING

The Martyrs' Square of Damascus had seen hundreds of hangings and death sentences, always before a stormy excited mob. Two months had not yet passed since the two American spies had been hanged in the same place, and now the square was again filled with bloodthirsty, vengeance-seeking masses.

"Death to Kamel! Death to the Zionist Spy!"

The slogans and shouts mingled in the darkness, creating a choking, hideous atmosphere.

Around the square the searchlights came on.

The execution ceremony was to be covered live from beginning to end by the Syrian TV network.

The Syrian top leadership attached great importance to the ceremony and its effect on the average Arab viewer.

The voice of the Radio Damascus announcer was positively gleeful. As the fateful moment approached, his voice got louder and louder. He shouted: "The Israeli spy Elie Cohn will be executed tonight! Death to the spy!"

Far from that stormy square, at the top of Hatehiya Street in Bat-Yam, Israel, a pale woman tensely followed every word on the radio, every scene on the TV screen. When the cry of revenge came from the Radio Damascus announcer, the words hit like a sledgehammer.

With the last of her strength, Nadia Cohn pounded the radio in front of her. Her fists smashed the glass and hurled the radio to the ground. Then, with a hysterical scream, she rushed at the windows and smashed all the window panes one after the other.

The condemned man's brothers, who had also followed the news, rushed over and held her. In vain the strong men tried to stop the woman who, for the last three months, had not left the radio—three long months of nightmare, with her heart nourishing the faint hope that maybe . . . maybe . . .

Now even this feeble hope dissolved in a sea of gnawing despair.

"Nothing did any good!" she wailed hysterically. "They wanted to see him dead!"

"Why did .they send my Elie?" elderly Sophie, Elie's mother, burst into tears. "Why did my son have to die among the Arabs?"

Suddenly the stream of tears stopped. Nadia burst over to the TV set and twisted the dial until the screen filled with the view of Al-Marjha Square.

"You mustn't look at that," one of the brothers whispered grimly.

"I must!" she cried. "Leave me alone! I must!"

The camera lenses focused on the police headquarters building, which was surrounded by policemen and soldiers.

At three thirty-five A.M., Damascus time, Elie was led out and brought to the scaffold under heavy guard.

The square seethed.

The fifty reporters and photographers permitted to be present were shocked; but they couldn't do a thing. They stood where they were, full of esteem for the hero who even in his last hour was proud, erect, calm.

The rows of soldiers made a living passageway to the scaffold.

Elie Cohn mounted the scaffold. The executioner placed the noose around his neck and waited for the signal. Then, in a fraction of a second, the base was removed from under Elie's feet and his body dangled at the end of the rope.

Four minutes later he was pronounced dead. Yet by order of the rulers of Damascus he remained hanging for another six hours, with his body wrapped in the white robe on display before the masses.

Only at nine A.M., Damascus time, was the body transferred to Damascus Central Hospital. It was not yet certain whether it would be permitted to be transported to Israel, or buried in the Jewish cemetery of Damascus.

After a lengthy debate in the Syrian Parliament, it was decided not to transfer the body despite all the appeals by Israel and influential elements the world over.

Elie Cohn was buried that afternoon in Damascus.

That day, May 18, 1965, Syria was in a turmoil. The West German ambassador in Damascus, Dr. Hans Manngold, left for Bonn. This followed Syria's official announcement, a week earlier, that she was severing diplomatic relations with Bonn because it had established relations with Israel.

As fate would have it, France—the country that had done more than any other to save Elie Cohn's life—was named to handle West Germany's affairs in Syria.

But the eyes of the world were not on the break between Syria and Germany. All tensely followed Israel's struggle for the return of the body of Elie Cohn to his country, and a proper burial.

Israel appealed to a friendly power in Europe and asked it to act in the matter. At the same time contact was made with the United Nations Observers Staff in Jerusalem, and General Odd Bull was required to act for the return of the body.

Meanwhile, expressions of grief and shock at the criminal deed of the Damascus authorities continued to pour in.

The Chief Rabbi of Damascus, Rabbi Nissim, published the following statement:

Humanity has suffered a grievous blow in seeing how in our day a government can transgress all laws of human sanctity, to maltreat a human being, oppress him with long and harsh torments, deny him the right to defend himself, and abuse his body after his death.

The divine commandment, *Thou shalt not suffer his cadaver to remain on the tree,* professed by the people of Israel and subsequently all humanity, has been profaned in the most frightful manner. It is the duty of everyone with breath in his nostrils and the spirit of life within him, to express his revulsion and disgust at this abominable act of murder, condonement of which would be not only a crime but encouragement of the forces of evil.

The people of Israel everywhere will pray for the soul of Eliyahu Ben Shaul Cohn, and for the end of sinners on the face of the earth. And I have forgiven, their blood I have not forgiven, and the Lord dwelleth in Zion.

Jacques Mercier, in a desperate attempt to compel the Syrians to return Elie Cohn's body, sent the following telegram to the head of the Syrian revolutionary council, General Amin El-Hafez:

> *By the urgent request of Mrs. Nadia Cohn, we request that the Syrian government forward to her Cohn's last letter, intended for his wife. We wish to know what steps should be taken in order to have Cohn's body returned to his family.*
>
> Advocate *Jacques Mercier*
> Advocate *Paul Arrighi*

It is unnecessary to point out that not one of the authorized persons in the Syrian Government took the trouble even to acknowledge the telegram—to say nothing of answering it.

Meanwhile, the shocked lawyers convened a meeting of the Parisian Council of Jurists and unrolled before them the web of lies woven by the Syrians in preventing them from defending Elie Cohn.

Subsequently, the Council of Jurists approved a sharply worded note to El-Hafez, protesting the "miscarriage of justice and the fraud" in the trial of Elie Cohn, wherein he was not provided suitable defense.

In a note published that day in Paris newspapers, the jurists denounced the Damascus procedures of justice "which are not those of a State of Law."

"There is no doubt," Jacques Mercier said, "that they tortured him to the point that there was no sense sending his body back to Israel. He was dead in body before he was dead in soul."

Then, remembering Dali's face, and the stupefied expression of the other top men, Mercier knew what Cohn had done to them and how great his achievement had been. He also knew that despite the fact that the Damascus rulers had had Elie tortured and in the end executed, deep in their hearts they were all full of admiration for the daring of the man, who had not been far from being a minister in their government.

Elie Cohn was a hero.

Even his enemies had to admit it.

The Arabs vs. Israel:
Twenty Years of Crisis

November 1947: The UN General Assembly (with Britain abstaining) votes to partition Palestine into Jewish and Arab states. The Arabs refuse to accept, vow to "push the Jews into the sea."

May 1948: David Ben-Gurion declares Israel's independence. The armies of Egypt, Jordan, Lebanon, Iraq, Syria, and contingents from Saudi Arabia invade the new state; hundreds of thousands of Arabs flee Palestine.

Mid-1949: A UN-sponsored truce ends the fighting. Jordan winds up with control of most of Arab Palestine, and Egypt with the Gaza Strip.

May 1950: The United States, Britain, and France issue a Tripartite Declaration guaranteeing the integrity of Arab and Israeli borders. But sporadic clashes between Arabs and Israelis continue along the frontiers.

April 1954: Colonel Nasser takes power in Egypt, harasses the British into agreeing to evacuate their military bases in the Suez Canal Zone.

September 1955: Finding his requests for arms turned down by the West, Nasser concludes an arms-for-cotton deal with Russia and Czechoslovakia.

July 1956: Alarmed by Nasser's arms deal with the Communists, the United States withdraws its offer to help build Egypt's Aswan High Dam. Nasser retaliates by nationalizing the Suez Canal.

October-November 1956: The British, French, and Israeli governments secretly plan coordinated action against Egypt. The Israelis attack first, driving through the Sinai Peninsula toward the Suez Canal. British and French troops then land at the canal's northern end. The Soviet Union threatens military action.

November-December 1956: Under United States and Soviet pressure, a cease-fire is agreed to and a 6,000-man United Nations Emergency Force is stationed in Egypt. Britain and France withdraw their forces.

January 1957: President Dwight D. Eisenhower reaffirms the United States guarantee of Mideast borders.

February 1957: The United States pledges to support Israel's right of free passage through the Strait of Tiran.

March 1957: Israel completes withdrawal from Gaza and the Strait of Tiran as UNEF takes position along the Israeli-Egyptian frontier.

July 1958: Civil war threatens Lebanon; Iraq's monarch is overthrown. At Lebanese request, United States marines land at Beirut; the British, fearing upheaval in Jordan, send troops to Amman. Both forces withdraw as the situation becomes more stable.

March 1960: Ben-Gurion declares Israel will divert water from the Jordan River to irrigate the Negev Desert. The Arabs threaten retaliation.

September 1962: A Nasser-backed revolution in Yemen ousts that country's monarchy. Civil war pits Saudi-Arabia-backed Yemeni monarchists against the new Republican government. An Egyptian expeditionary force, now totaling about 40,000 men, enters Yemen to aid the Republicans.

May 1963: President John F. Kennedy reaffirms United

States support for the territorial integrity of both Israel and its neighbors in the Mideast.

May 1964: Israelis begin diverting Jordan River waters at the Sea of Galilee. The Arabs attempt to organize a Jordan River diversion plan of their own.

February 1966: The extremist wing of Socialist Baath Party seizes power in a Syrian military coup; its militant leaders offer backing to a terrorist group which carries out a campaign of sabotage along the Syrian-Israeli frontier.

August 1966: President Johnson reaffirms the United States guarantee of Mideastern borders.

November 1966: Syria and Egypt sign a mutual-defense agreement, establishing a joint military command. Faced with continuing Arab sabotage and harassment, Israeli army units raid a Jordanian village. The UN Security Council censures Israel.

May 1967: Syrian-Israeli clashes continue through winter and into spring, culminating in an air battle in which six Syrian MIG's are destroyed. Israeli Prime Minister Eshkol threatens retaliation if Syrian terrorism continues.

June 1967: Supported by excellent intelligence reports and quick and devastating air attacks, Israel defeats the combined Arab armies on all fronts in the lightning Six-Day War.

1968-1969: Sporadic clashes continue to occur along the Israeli borders as the UN strives hard to find a peace solution for the long-troubled Middle East. Iraq's public hangings of Jews and others accused of being "Israeli spies" cause worldwide protests.